RE-READING

LITERATURE

NEW CRITICAL APPROACHES
TO THE STUDY OF ENGLISH

Sue Hackman and Barbara Marshall

Hodder & Stoughton

LONDON SYDNEY AUCKLAND TORONTO

Cover illustrator: Sarah Ball

ISBN 0 340 51233 4

First published 1990

© 1990 Sue Hackman and Barbara Marshall

Typeset by Wearside Tradespools, Fulwell, Sunderland
Printed for the educational publishing division of Hodder and Stoughton
Ltd, Mill Road, Dunton Green, Sevenoaks, Kent by St Edmundsbury
Press, Bury St Edmunds, Suffolk

CONTENTS

ACKNOWLEDGMENTS

The publishers would like to thank the following for permission to reproduce material in this volume:

Katherine Allingham for the extracts from *The Dukinfield I Knew* by James Brooke, published by Neil Richardson; the Associated Press for the aerial photo of Hiroshima; William Bealby-Wright for his poem 'The Wordsworths'; Bloodaxe Books for the extract from 'V' by Tony Harrison, published by Bloodaxe Books (1989); Jonathan Cape Ltd/Phoebe Larmore on behalf of Margaret Atwood for 'Happy Endings' by Margaret Atwood from Hermione Lee (ed) *The Secret Self* (1985) and *Murder In The Dark* (1983); Jonathan Cape Ltd for extracts from *Love On The Dole* by Walter Greenwood (1933), *Taking It Like A Woman* by Annie Oatley (1984) and 'The New Fast Automatic Daffodils' by Adrian Henri from Roger McGough (ed) *Strictly Private*, Kestrel, 1981; Carcanet Press Ltd/New Directions Publicity Corporation for 'Self Portrait' by William Carlos Williams from *Pictures from Breughel: Collected Poems 1950–1962* (1987); Century Hutchinson Ltd for 'Manwatching' by Georgina Garrett from Michael Rosen (ed) *I See A Voice* (1982); Chatto and Windus/The Hogarth Press for 'Speech for Alternative Creation' by James Berry and 'Talk, Talk: Nigger Talk Talk' by Jimi Rand from James Berry (ed) *News From Babylon* (1984); William Collins Sons and Co Ltd for the extract from *Evil Under The Sun* by Agatha Christie Mallowen (1940, 1941); Curtis Brown London on behalf of John Wain for 'Au Jardin des Plantes' by John Wain from *Weep Before God* published by Macmillan; Danjaq SA and United Artists Company for the Gun Logo Symbol (1962); M C Escher Heirs/Cordon Art, Baarn, Holland for 'Drawing Hands' by Escher (1989); Faber and Faber Ltd for 'Cantos IV' from *The Cantos of Ezra Pound* (1987), Hugh Selwyn Mauberley from *Collected Shorter Poems* by Ezra Pound (1984), extracts from *Dogg's Hamlet, Cahout's Macbeth* by Tom Stoppard (1980), extracts from *The Burning Book* by Maggie Gee (1983), 'Nothing to be Said' from *The Whitsun Weddings* by Philip Larkin (1964) and *Not I* by Samuel Beckett (1984); Alison Fell for her poem 'August 6, 1948' from Linda Hoy (ed) *Poems For Peace*, Pluto (1986); Glidrose Productions/Ian Fleming for the extract from *The Spy Who Loved Me* by Ian Fleming published by Jonathan Cape (1962); Rupert Goodwins for his article 'The Power of Infection', *The Guardian* April 1988; Tony Harrison for 'Them and Uz' and 'The Queen's English' both from *Selected Poems*, Penguin (1984); Heinemann Educational Books Ltd for extracts from *The Critical Sense* by James Reeves (1956) and *Six Characters In Search of An Author* by Luigi Pirandello, translated by Frederick May (1954); HMSO for the Cryptic Crossword from *The Independent* 30 August, 1989; IPC Magazines for the extract from the magazine digest of *Haunted* by James Herbert, published in *Woman* 23 March, 1988; the Kunsthistorisches Museum, Vienna, for *The Peasant Wedding*, by Breughel; Tom Leonard for his poem 'Unrelated Incidents'; MacDonald Children's Books for the extract from *MacDonald Starters: Food*; Macmillan Inc for the two drawings by Rausch from *En Masse*, Collier Books, a division of Macmillan Inc (1975); the Mansell Collection for *The Lecture* by Hogarth; Marvell Press for 'Wires' by Philip Larkin from *The Less Deceived* (1955); Methuen London for 'Women's entry into culture is experienced as a lack' and 'Middle-Class Hero' by Michele Roberts from *The Mirror of The Mother* by the same author; The Observer Ltd for the articles re: Down the Road Worlds Away and re: SARUM book covers both 1987 and the cover of Section 5 of *The Observer* 9 April, 1989; Penguin Books Ltd/Alfred A Knopf Inc for the extract from *Hiroshima* by John Hersey (1986), The New Yorker (1946) and 'A Third World War Poem' by Bill Greenwell, Viking (1986); Secker and Warburg for the translation of 'An Everyday Occurence' by Franz Kafka (1973); May Swenson for her translation from Swedish of 'Under a Ramshackle Rainbow' by Ingemar Gustafson from *Half Sun Half Sleep* (1967); Times Newspapers Ltd for the extract from Margaret Thatcher's Conference Speech, *The Times* 11 October, 1989; John Tomsett for his poem 'Mothering Sundays' with drafts and commentary; the Trustees of the British Museum for *The Lecture* by Hogarth; Virago Press for 'Significant Moments in the Life of My Mother' by Margaret Atwood from *Bluebeard's Egg* by the same author (1988); Mrs Theresa Whistler for 'Mortal Combat' by Mary Coleridge from T Whistler (ed) *The Collected Poems of Mary Coleridge*, Rupert Hart-Davis (1954); The Women's Press Ltd for extracts from *The Visitation* by Michele Roberts (1983) and 'My Man Bovanne' from *Gorilla My Love* by Toni Cade Bambara (1984)

TO THE TEACHER

One can no longer speak of a 'new' critical theory: it has been established for many years on the continent and also in British universities. Now school syllabuses are rethinking their approach to literature. In this book we have collected together some of the material and approaches we have found successful with students aged 16–19. We have tried to bridge the leap from the traditions of practical criticism into modern theory in a way which will make sense in the classroom. Inevitably we have made simplifications and omissions. Most of these arise out of the constraints of textbooks: money, space, the limits of the written word. Most of the issues covered in the book are relevant to texts in other media such as film, television and drama. These media have suffered in the past from being taught as pseudo-books, and we hope teachers will use ideas from this book to study them in their intended form.

We have arranged the book into chapters and sections for convenience, but there is no 'body of knowledge' which offers itself for piecemeal consumption. Every chapter has a bearing on the others. We hope therefore that teachers will feel free to select and adapt our own order to suit the inclinations and interests of their classes and themselves.

We wish to record our thanks to Wink and Chris who babysat and proffered advice while we wrote the book, and to Andrew Steeds and Rosalind Scott at Hodder & Stoughton for their work on the manuscript. The book is dedicated to Sally and Stephen who were conceived, carried and born during its production.

Sue Hackman & Barbara Marshall

Designed by Wm Hogarth

WHO OWNS LANGUAGE?

The Literary

Establishment

THE AMALGAMATED UNIVERSITIES EXAMINATION BOARD

General Certificate of Education – Advanced Level June Examination

ENGLISH LITERATURE – 965/4

Paper 1

Thursday, 5 June, 9.30 a.m. to 10.45 p.m.

1 hour and 15 minutes allowed

You are advised to spend about 15 minutes in reading the paper before you begin to write.

A. Read the following poem carefully and write a critical appreciation so as to bring out what you feel to be its distinctive qualities.

(40 marks)

First Love

I ne'er was struck before that hour
   With love so sudden and so sweet.
Her face it bloomed like a sweet flower
   And stole my heart away complete.
My face turned pale as deadly pale,
   My legs refused to walk away,
And when she looked 'what could I ail?'
   My life and all seemed turned to clay.

And then my blood rushed to my face
   And took my sight away.
The trees and bushes round the place
   Seemed midnight at noonday.
I could not see a single thing,
   Words from my eyes did start;
They spoke as chords do from the string,
   And blood burnt round my heart.

Are flowers the winter's choice?
   Is love's bed always snow?
She seemed to hear my silent voice
   And love's appeal to know.
I never saw so sweet a face
   As that I stood before:
My heart has left its dwelling place
   And can return no more.

John Clare

WHAT IS LITERATURE?

One of the main aims of this book is to offer some considerations of the complex ways through which meaning is made. It is interesting to start by considering some of the assumptions made by this examination paper.

The question seems open-ended. However, the task of a 'critical appreciation' assumes that you will think about the poem in certain ways: indeed if you are used to this kind of exercise, you may already have a checklist in your mind of what to comment on. You are expected to recognise that it would be appropriate to comment on the poem's imagery or form for example, and possibly to include your personal reactions. The language of the rubric ('its distinctive qualities', 'appreciation') also assumes that you recognise that poetry is worth writing about and that you are prepared to enter into a 'discourse' about this poem as a piece of 'Literature'.

What is literature? There will always be problems in defining it. The very broadest definition of 'anything written' will not do: that would include shopping lists but not oral poetry or drama in performance. Whatever attempts are made to define literature, they inevitably end up by talking about it in terms of its value. A teenage magazine might have significance of a cultural kind, or a car manual of a practical kind, but literature is, *by its very nature*, important, because it is believed to be 'good'. Who decides which works qualify as literature and which do not? This question, which it has often been considered the task of literary criticism to answer, goes a long way towards answering the first question: what is literature?

● *As one of the editors of the anthology* The Great Love Poems of English Literature, *you are invited to consider the following poems for inclusion in your book. Selection will be finalised at an editorial group meeting. Prepare notes on the poems and list them in order of suitability.*

POEM 1

Of all the girls that are so smart
    There's none like pretty Sally;
She is the darling of my heart,
    And she lives in our alley.
There is no lady in the land
    Is half so sweet as Sally;
She is the darling of my heart,
    And she lives in our alley.

Her father he makes cabbage-nets,
    And through the streets does cry 'em;
Her mother she sells laces long
    To such as please to buy 'em:
But sure such folks could ne'er beget
    So sweet a girl as Sally!
She is the darling of my heart,
    And she lives in our alley.

When she is by, I leave my work,
    I love her so sincerely;
My master comes like any Turk,
    And bangs me most severely:
But let him bang his bellyful,
    I'll bear it all for Sally;
She is the darling of my heart,
    And she lives in our alley.

Of all the days that's in the week
    I dearly love but one day –
And that's the day that comes betwixt
    A Saturday and Monday;
For then I'm dressed all in my best
    To walk abroad with Sally;
She is the darling of my heart,
    And she lives in our alley.

My master carries me to church,
    And often am I blamèd
Because I leave him in the lurch
    As soon as text is namèd;
I leave the church in sermon-time
    And slink away to Sally;
She is the darling of my heart,
    And she lives in our alley.

When Christmas comes about again,
 O, then I shall have money;
I'll hoard it up, and box it all,
 I'll give it to my honey:
I would it were ten thousand pound,
 I'd give it all to Sally;
She is the darling of my heart,
 And she lives in our alley.

My master and the neighbours all,
 Make game of me and Sally,
And, but for her, I'd better be
 A slave and row a galley;
But when my seven long years are out,
 O, then I'll marry Sally;
O, then we'll wed, and then we'll bed –
 But not in our alley!

―――――――――

POEM 2

She walks in beauty, like the night
 Of cloudless climes and starry skies;
And all that's best of dark and bright
 Meet in her aspect and her eyes:
Thus mellowed to that tender light
 Which heaven to gaudy day denies.

One shade the more, one ray the less,
 Had half impaired the nameless grace
Which waves in every raven tress,
 Or softly lightens o'er her face;
Where thoughts serenely sweet express
 How pure, how dear their dwelling place.

And on that cheek, and o'er that brow,
 So soft, so calm, yet eloquent,
The smiles that win, the tints that glow,
 But tell of days in goodness spent,
A mind at peace with all below,
 A heart whose love is innocent!

POEM 3

One day I wrote her name upon the strand,
  But came the waves and washèd it away:
Again I wrote it with a second hand,
  But came the tide, and made my pains his prey.
'Vain man,' said she, 'thou do'st in vain assay,
  A mortal thing so to immortalize,
For I myself shall like to this decay,
  And eek my name be wipèd out likewise.'
'Not so,' quoth I, 'let baser things devise
  To die in dust, but you shall live by fame:
My verse your virtues rare shall eternize,
  And in the heavens write your glorious name,
    Where, whenas death shall all the world subdue,
    Our love shall live, and later life renew.'

————————

POEM 4

From across the party I watch you,
Watching her.
Do my possessive eyes
Imagine your silent messages?
I think not.
She looks across at you
And telegraphs her flirtatious reply.
I have come to recognize this code,
You are on intimate terms with this pretty stranger,
And there is nothing I can do,
My face is calm, expressionless,
But my eyes burn into your back.
While my insides shout with rage.
She weaves her way towards you,
Turning on a bewitching smile.
I can't see your face, but you are mesmerised I expect.
I can predict you: I know this scene so well,
Some acquaintance grabs your arm,
You turn and meet my accusing stare head on,
Her eyes follow yours, meet mine,
And then slide away, she understands,
She's not interested enough to compete.
It's over now.
She fades away, you drift towards me,
'I'm bored' you say, without a trace of guilt,
So we go.

Passing the girl in the hall.
'Bye' I say frostily,
I suppose
You winked.

- *In a group discuss the poems and select two for inclusion.*
- *What factors did you consider in making your own judgements and how do your criteria compare with those of other members in your group?*
- *Once you have completed the exercise, look at the end of the chapter, where you will find the titles and writers of these poems.*

It's quite possible that there was considerable consensus among your group of students about the criteria for selection, but if you found yourself in disagreement over the ranking of the poems or if you were unsettled by the identity of the poets, you might assume this is because you are not experienced enough, not yet a 'proper critic'. And being or becoming a 'proper critic' involves the refinement of the twin activities of appreciation and judgement: first you are expected to understand and explain a text, then and only then you may comment on its overall value and 'place' it in terms of its literary worth. The notion of a 'proper critic' is itself worth questioning. This is not to say that it is wrong to judge writing but perhaps we need to question whether criticism, the simple art of appreciating good literature, is quite as simple and innocent as it might seem.

THE CRITICISM OF LITERATURE

- *What is literary criticism and where would you expect to encounter it? Compile a list of examples and say what the purposes of each one are.*

Literary study developed from a largely leisurely pursuit in the nineteenth century to an academic and professional occupation in the late nineteenth and twentieth century as English Literature courses proliferated. The status of literary criticism, however, remains ambiguous. Some people are hostile to the notion of criticism and see it as destructive to the enjoyment of writing, or as a parasite feeding off literature. It is certainly the case that literary criticism could not exist without literature. However it may also be true that literature has depended on criticism to build it into an important feature of our culture. Argued from this perspective, criticism constructs a framework within which we can sensibly examine literature and draws into it those texts which qualify as literature, leaving others outside.

The extracts which follow give the views of two very famous critics from the period in which literary study was establishing itself: the first brief quotation is from Matthew Arnold writing in the second half of the nineteenth century; the second is from F. R. Leavis' famous book on the English Novel, published in 1948:

1 I am bound by my own definition of criticism: a disinterested endeavour to learn and propagate the best that is known and thought in the world.

Matthew Arnold

2 The great English novelists are Jane Austen, George Eliot, Henry James and Joseph Conrad – to stop for the moment at that comparatively safe point in history . . .

The only way to escape misrepresentation is never to commit oneself to any critical judgement that makes an impact – that is, never to say anything. I still, however think that the best way to promote profitable discussion is to be as clear as possible with oneself about what one sees and judges, to try and establish the essential discriminations in the given field of interest, and to state them as clearly as one can (for disagreement, if necessary). And it seems to me that in the field of fiction some challenging discriminations are very much called for; the field is so large and offers such insidious temptations to complacent confusions of judgement and to critical indolence. It is of the field of fiction belonging to Literature that I am thinking, and I am thinking in particular of the present vogue of the Victorian age. Trollope, Charlotte Yonge, Mrs Gaskell, Wilkie Collins, Charles Reade, Charles and Henry Kingsley, Marryat, Shorthouse – one after another the minor novelists of that period are being commended to our attention, written up, and publicised by broadcast, and there is a marked tendency to suggest that they not only have various kinds of interest to offer but that they are living classics. (Are they not all in the literary histories?) There are Jane Austen, Mrs Gaskell, Scott, 'the Brontës', Dickens, Thackeray, George Eliot, Trollope and so on, all, one gathers, classical novelists.

It is necessary to insist, then, that there are important distinctions to be made, and that far from all of the names in the literary histories really belong to the realm of significant creative achievement. And as a recall to a due sense of differences it is well to start by distinguishing the few really great – the major novelists who count in the same way as the major poets, in the sense that they not only change the possibilities of the art for practitioners and readers, but that they are significant in terms of the human awareness they promote; awareness of the possibilities of life.

(from *The Great Tradition* by F. R. Leavis)

- *Underline the words or phrases that seem to make the most significant statement about criticism.*
- *What views of literature and of critical practice underlie these comments?*

The following passage is taken from a book containing numerous examples of how to criticise a poem. It considers the poem by John Clare that you discussed at the beginning of this chapter. Read the poem again, then read this interpretation:

Earlier in this chapter reference has been made to John Clare, an almost uneducated labourer from a Northamptonshire village whose ruling passion, throughout life, was poetry. He was a man of the countryside, living among the poorest villagers, intimate with rural nature, and writing, like Wordsworth's idealized poet, 'in a selection of the language really used by men'. Like the child in Robert Graves's poem 'The Cool Web', Clare was a man of extreme sensibility, acutely aware of his surroundings and rendered almost helpless by emotion. He was not, like the child, dumb; his feelings burst out into spontaneous poetry.

Now we cannot expect spontaneous poetry to be technically excellent. 'Kubla Khan', if we accept Coleridge's account of its origin, is a brilliant exception. We expect it, above all, to express pure emotion, free from artistic 'working up' and revision; we expect it to be alive with feeling; when the writer is ill-educated, as Clare was, and scarcely literate except in verse, we can expect simplicity, directness and truth. These are the characteristics of 'First Love'. Clare's aim is to give as truthful a statement of his feelings as possible on first falling in love. In verse 1 he uses the image of a flower to express the effect that the face of the girl had upon him; he goes on to describe the sense of paralysis that her beauty caused him. Verse 2 tells of a feeling almost of suffocation and blindness.

> 'I could not see a single thing,
> Words from my eyes did start.'

The meaning of this statement is plain; the form of it is original and surprising. It is referred to again in verse 3:

> 'She seemed to hear my silent voice
> And love's appeal to know.'

The silent voice is the appeal that has come from his blinded eyes. The best he can do to express the sense of this silent appeal is the riddle:

> 'Are flowers the winter's choice?
> Is love's bed always snow?'

The lines are metrically defective, and obviously unrevised; their composition was apparently inspired – Clare could not have worked out logically what he was saying. Winter is the time for snow, love's bed the place for flowers. Must these positions be reversed? he asks. Must love be unfulfilled like flowers born to waste in winter? After this, the remaining four lines seem somewhat trite, and they do not follow inevitably from what precedes them. Technically it is a far from perfect poem; it has flaws of structure and diction, but not of taste or feeling. It needs revision. The title does not seem to have been fully considered; what Clare means is perhaps Love at First

Sight, not First Love. Yet we cannot doubt the essential truth of the poem. It describes with almost unequalled closeness an emotion – a psychological incident almost impossible to describe without sentimentality or false touches. It bears out Wordsworth's belief that those most closely in touch with nature experience emotion more purely and intensely than those with a more sophisticated way of life. Love, poetry, and nature composed almost the whole of Clare's existence. There never was a poet more intimate with nature; he remained her rapturous adorer all his life. To him the music which was assured of immortality was not the songs of men, the sound of human voices, or words in books; it was the music of nature. This is not an original thought; it is not, in itself, a profound thought. It is scarcely a thought at all.

(from *The Critical Sense* by James Reeves)

- *What aspects of poetry has this commentator focused on?*
- *What assumptions does he make about poetry?*
- *What attitudes to poetry do you think this writer holds and how far do you agree with them?*

As we have said earlier, the significance attached to literature (and to literary study) grew at the end of the nineteenth century (a fact some people have put down to the decline of religious faith). People had of course always written about literature but as they began to do so in greater numbers, demand grew for a more rigorous approach to be taken to literary study, something that seemed more as if it was applying a method and less like indulging in a good read. 'Practical criticism' seemed one answer: this involved scrutinising a text closely, and examining its language and form to arrive at an understanding of the piece. This may well be a familiar practice to you; it is certainly very convenient for schools and colleges because it does not require any wider knowledge that that of the process – imagery, rhyme and so on. It also suggests itself as somehow pure and objective, because it is apparently a direct encounter between the reader and the words on the page. However, many critics and teachers do not believe it is quite as simple as it seems.

There are nowadays a great many different ways to approach literary study: practical criticism no longer holds total sway as it did previously. Some of these newer approaches fall neatly into certain schools of thought; many do not. For example, a historical approach will examine the social background to the text while a Marxist approach will consider how the text and also meaning in general are produced in relation to historical and political forces; a structuralist approach would concentrate on the pattern of the parts that make up the text rather than discuss its meaning; a psychoanalytic approach might be interested in uncovering the unconscious processes at work in writing or reading the text, while a feminist approach might consider the politics of gender in relationship to the text or the literary tradition generally. It is very difficult to simplify these approaches without misrepresenting them. One of our aims in this book is to consider the complex ways in which meaning is made rather than suggest that a text can be dealt with in simple categories of character, narrative, style, form and theme.

- *Try writing an interpretation of the poem 'First Love' that offers a very different reading from the one presented by James Reeves – for example from a feminist's, psychoanalyst's or Marxist's viewpoint, or by a detailed consideration of the grammar and structure of the poem.*

THE EDUCATIONAL ESTABLISHMENT

The study of literature in schools and colleges is determined by many factors which include: tradition, the kind of people who become literature teachers, the methods of examination, the nature of the examination boards, and university places for which 'successful' students compete. For many years the universities dominated the examination boards (Practical Criticism, for example, was largely a 'product' of Cambridge University) and the role of A level in particular was to groom future students. But as more people study and read literature for reasons other than going on to read it at university, and as literary theory develops, changes in the examination system can be expected.

The favourite literary theories of the universities were – and still are – very influential in schools. The questions set in examination papers and which are popular with literature teachers – themselves successful products of the system – reveal the philosophies which guide their thinking, as our account of the opening examination paper indicated.

- *Consider the following questions which have appeared in this or a very similar form in examination papers and coursework folders in recent years. What views of literature and learning are implied in them?*

Choose any two of Hamlet's soliloquies and by close reference to the language and thought expressed in them, say what they reveal about his state of mind at those particular points in the play.

- *What assumptions does this question make about the way drama should be studied? What does it suggest about the way characters should be interpreted? What sort of study techniques does it require of the student?*

Imagine you have been invited to direct the play *Hamlet*. Prior to rehearsals for Act III, Scene iv, you are approached by the actors playing Gertrude, Hamlet and the ghost of Old Hamlet for guidance about the way you want them to approach their parts. Prepare a briefing document explaining your interpretation of this scene and give specific guidance to the actors about their behaviour and delivery.

- *What assumptions does this question make about the way drama should be studied? What does it suggest about the way characters should be viewed? What sort of study techniques does it require of the student?*

Choose any two characters in the novel *Emma* who are present at the Box Hill outing (Chapter 43) and write their diary entries for that evening, reviewing the events of the outing and their reactions to them, and articulating their major concerns at this point in time.

- *What assumptions does this question make about the way characters should be viewed? What sort of reading does it call for from the student?*

Discuss the role of Fate in *Tess of the D'Urbervilles.*

- *What expectations does this question have about the nature of 'discussion'? What does it imply about the composition and intention of novels? And what approach to the text does it oblige students to take?*

Write an extra twenty lines in the style of Chaucer's prologue to *The Canterbury Tales* introducing a further character into the band of pilgrims.

- *What is the status of the text in this question and what assumptions does it make about the way readers respond to texts? What benefits and limitations might a student experience in answering such a question?*

Re-read the opening chapter of *Great Expectations* and consider your reactions as you read it. What interest does it hold for you and what expectations does it raise? How effective do you find it as an opening?

- *What assumptions does this question make about the role of the reader? What does it assume about the student's past encounter with the text?*
- *Look back over some of your own assignment titles and consider what views of literature and learning are implied in them.*
- *Consider the method by which you will be examined at the end of the course. What implications does it have for the type of work set and the way you will approach it?*

THE PUBLISHING INDUSTRY

Publishing companies commission writers to produce manuscripts which they then prepare for publication. Their work includes commissioning, editing, printing and marketing. The publishing industry in this country is a commercial business, so one important consideration in the commissioning and marketing of books is whether they will yield a profit.

Market pressures influence what is published and, therefore, what literature will be available to the public. Much that is written is rejected by publishers. Much of this may not be bad: it may simply be uncommercial. Publishers also, however, have to be alert to new talent, and they have an important role in identifying the writers who will eventually become established authors. This may involve commercial risks. James Joyce's novel *Ulysses* was rejected by several publishers before it was accepted and published by Shakespeare and Company, Paris in 1922: it has since become a 'classic'.

Publishers also control the publication of literary criticism and educational books, and so they play an important role in framing the outlook of the next generation.

- *Put yourself in the position of publisher and consider the issues raised in the following cases:*

1 One of your best-selling authors has offered you a manuscript which has little literary merit. What considerations would you make in deciding whether or not to publish it?

2 You have struck a lucrative market by selling simplified versions of examination texts, which are scorned by educationalists but which sell well. What issues are at stake?

3 You work for a reputable publishing house specialising in modern classics, whose profits are reliable. Over recent years, there has been disquiet that no new writers of quality seem to be emerging and that the output of your older authors is tailing off. Where might the problem lie and what strategies would you employ to deal with it?

4 You are responsible for promoting a new line of books by gay writers. Sales are adequate to cover costs, but not as good as you had hoped. A market survey reveals that the books are reaching committed gay readers, but are being ignored by others who see the subject as irrelevant to them, and positively rejected by still others who see the subject as distasteful. In other words, you seem to be preaching to the converted. In attempting to boost sales and bearing in mind your modest budget, what sort of promotion strategy would you adopt?

An appealing cover or provocative blurb can attract readers, and so marketing is an important aspect of selling books. Look at the cover designs on page 16 which were all used for the novel *Sarum* by Edward Rutherford.

- *Discuss the variety of ways in which the jackets may be appealing to potential readers.*
- *Can you identify the books of particular publishers, series and marketing campaigns? What is distinctive about their presentation? Are you aware of publishers specialising in particular types of book?*
- *Take a novel or anthology you know well and design alternative covers and blurbs for it, before writing an explanatory note about each one. Are any or all of the versions a true representation of the text?*

Reading List

The Rise of The Novel by Ian Watt (Hogarth Press, 1987) opens with an interesting account of the forces which made novels a commodity.
The Function of Criticism by Terry Eagleton (Verso Editions, 1984) is a challenging account of the role and history of the criticism industry.
The Preachers of Culture by Margaret Mathieson (Allen and Unwin, 1975) discusses the development of English teaching and its values.
Twentieth Century Literary Criticism by David Lodge (Longman, 1972) is an anthology of different approaches.
Small World by David Lodge (Secker and Warburg, 1984) is a novel about university critics on conferences which English teachers find amusing. There's a funny but fair burlesque of modern critical theories in Part 5 in case your teacher scorns to simplify.

The Anthology Poems from 'What is Literature?'
1 *Sally In Our Alley* by Henry Carey
2 *She Walks In Beauty* by Lord Byron
3 *One Day I Wrote Her Name Upon The Strand* by Edmund Spenser
4 *Manwatching* by Georgia Garrett
Poems 1–3 can be found in *The Penguin Book of Love Poetry* edited by Jon
Stallworthy (Penguin, 1976)

FINDING A VOICE

BLACK AND WHITE

● *Read the following passage from* Gone With the Wind, *a novel written in the 1930s and set in the southern states of America during the civil war, and consider the portrayal of the servant Mammy:*

Mammy emerged from the hall, a huge old woman with the small, shrewd eyes of an elephant. She was shining black, pure African, devoted to her last drop of blood to the O'Haras, Ellen's mainstay, the despair of her three daughters, the terror of the other house servants. Mammy was black, but her code of conduct and her sense of pride were as high or higher than those of her owners. She had been raised in the bedroom of Solange Robillard, Ellen O'Hara's mother, a dainty, cold-nosed Frenchwoman, who spared neither her children nor her servants their just punishment for any infringement of decorum. She had been Ellen's mammy and had come with her from Savannah to the up-country when she married. Whom Mammy loved, she chastened. And as her love for Scarlett and her pride in her were enormous, the chastening process was practically continuous.

'Is de gempmum gone? Huccome you din' ast dem ter stay fer supper, Miss Scarlett? Ah done tole Poke ter lay two extry plates fer dem. Whar's yo' manners?'

'Oh, I was so tired of hearing them talk about the war that I couldn't have endured it through supper, especially with Pa joining in and shouting about Mr Lincoln.'

'You ain' got no mo' manners dan a fe'el han', an' affer Miss Ellen an' me done laboured wid you. An' hyah you is widout yo' shawl! An' de night air fixin' ter set in! Ah done tole you an' tole you 'bout gittin' fever frum settin' in de night air wid nuthin' on yo' shoulders. Come on in de house, Miss Scarlett.'

Scarlett turned away from Mammy with studied nonchalance, thankful that her face had been unnoticed in Mammy's preoccupation with the matter of the shawl.

'No, I want to sit here and watch the sunset. It's so pretty. You run get my shawl. Please, Mammy, and I'll sit here till Pa comes home.'

'Yo' voice soun' lak you catchin' a cole,' said Mammy suspiciously.

'Well, I'm not,' said Scarlett impatiently. 'You fetch me my shawl.'

Mammy waddled back into the hall and Scarlett heard her call softly up the stairwell to the upstairs maid.

'You, Rosa! Drap me Miss Scarlett's shawl!' Then, more loudly: 'Wuthless nigger! She ain' never whar she does nobody no good. Now, Ah got ter climb up an' git it mahseff.'

(from *Gone With the Wind* by Margaret Mitchell)

- *What impression does the reader get of Mammy's character and position?*
- *How far is this impression derived from the language describing her and through her own speech?*
- *What view of black people are we invited to share here?*

RACE AND LANGUAGE

I understood him in many things, and let him know I was very well pleased with him; in a little time I began to speak with him and teach him to speak to me; and first I made him know his name should be Friday, which was the day I saved his life; I called him so for the memory of the time; I likewise taught him to say Master, and then let him know, that was to be my name; I likewise taught him to say yes and no, and to know the meaning of them . . .

(from *Robinson Crusoe* by Daniel Defoe)

When Robinson Crusoe starts to teach Friday the English language he says it is in order for him 'to know the meaning'. This is more than just being able to put names to things, it also involves understanding his position: one of his first words is to name 'Master'. As we suggest in the chapter on gender, language helps to fix people in their place in society. This is particularly true where one country takes over another, and a new language is imposed on people and their native language is suppressed. A new language imposes and symbolises authority and prevents the colonised groups from using their original language to organise themselves to rebel. British slave-traders and others from the seventeenth century to the nineteenth century made efforts to see that groups of Black African slaves speaking the same language were separated, often chaining together slaves on plantations in pairs who were unable to communicate. An example closer to home might be Northern Ireland earlier this century where the British Commissioners responsible for education tried to ensure that the Irish language would die out as quickly as possible in the province's schools.

Even when a colonising power leaves and returns the land to its original people, it often leaves its language as a political legacy, as Derek Walcott suggests in one of his poems:

It is good that everything's gone, except their language
Which is everything.

The West Indians from the Caribbean still use the English language, but it can be in a form influenced by other groups who dominated them (such as French, Spanish, Dutch and Portuguese) and also by the words and rhythms of their original African languages. Such a language might be identified separately as, for example, patois, Creole or Black British English. For writers from such a background, choosing language is not a simple issue: should it be the language of the 'Master', or some form which subverts that language to create a new identity for themselves? If an original language is available, such as Irish, Welsh or an African language, what implications will this have for the writer?

- *Read the following poems which were written by West Indian writers and consider the ways they approach the problems of language:*

I   SPEECH FOR ALTERNATIVE CREATION

Let us recreate all things in our own image.
Let us make a new beginning.
Let us remove night, dawn, dusk,
remove black thunder, leave lightning,
dismiss Dark November, leave
all eyes on noon, that dazzle
of summer, our white heat of days.

Let us remove the Dark Continent,
and be humane to drifters.
Let us build up a government Blackmale list
and a Blacklist of Blacklegs
for a kind and natural exile use.
Let there be no tar to dip the brush in,
though twin adjectives Big and Black can stay,
to be own reliable terror image.

Let us remember: Blackmarks have a way
of coming to walk like children.
Let us remember this:
each boy our own, each girl,
is our own support garrison.

We shall let it be law, that anything
except immaculate conception
is Miscegenation, that no
white lady shall ride a black stallion,
that all raven-haired people be made
white-haired, all black Bibles be cancelled
for white ones, and that pure milk
shall replace all coffee drinking.

We shall get every Blacksheep into
a straight scapegoat, and be clear
that no Blackguard can ever be fair.
We shall erase, correct out, every printed word,
have pure pages to show decent minds,
Even trains shall have no tunnels to go
through. We shall make all our roads into
journeys on silver. And our science
shall treat all brown earth till changed,
like beauty of clinical cottonwool.

Afterall, a non-white thing is a non-thing;
Might as well will it away.

Let us deport devildom. Let us have
that dreamed of constant world, mirroring
the sun with white lands and houses and walls.
Let us make it all a marvel of a moonshine.

James Berry

2   TALK, TALK: NIGGER TALK TALK

Listen na, is me turn to talk now ya know
Ahna gwine hav ahna turn later.
So sit down and let me talk na.
Let we rap togedder.
    All we gwine talk: talk nigger talk.
Me hope ya can understan I
Cause me no talk no London talk
    Me no talk no Europe talk
    Me talking black, nigger talk;
    Funky talk
    Nitty gritty grass-root talk.
Das what I da talk
So if ahna don't like nigger talk
Ga!
Ga na, wha ahna wait fa?
Ga!
Ma no mek na apology.
Me gwine talk it, like it is.
If ahna got soul
    Ahna gwine listen.

If ya black, ya dig it.
If ya is a nigger
    Ya gwine talk it
But if ya coloured, ah know ya don't wan it.
Fa is talk, talk, nigger talk:
Dat's what I da talk
Cause de talk is togedder talk,
Like right on, out-a-sight, kind-a-too-much.
Ya hip to it yat?

Ya dig de funky way to talk
Talk, talk?
Dis na white talk:
Na white talk dis.
It is coon, nignog, samba wog talk;
Sweetsweet talk.
Na pussyfooting talk dis.
Ya talk: 'pickeny, boogie, lickshe, bigfoot,
Wabine, putop, is wha dat?'
Can ya talk, talk talk?
Na Tom talk
Na liberal talk
Na grammar talk
Na big word talk
Na high up talk:
People talk
Black people talk
Black, nigger people talk.
Can ya talk it
Dis talk talk
Nigger talk talk?
Can ya?
Can ya talk
Nigger
Talk talk?

Jimi Rand

- *To whom are the poems addressed?*
- *What kinds of language has the poet chosen to use in each case and how closely related is this to standard English?*
- *What dangers and what benefits do you think there might be in using a vernacular such as Rand does here? Is more or less 'communicated'?*

RECLAIMING A VOICE

- *Read the following complete short story* My Man Bovanne *by the American writer, Toni Cade Bambara, and consider the ways she presents her central character and the issues of black identity and language:*

Blind people got a hummin jones if you notice. Which is understandable completely once you been around one and notice what no eyes will force you into to see people, and you get past the first time, which seems to come out of nowhere, and it's like you in church again with fat-chest ladies and old gents gruntin a hum low in the throat to whatever the preacher be saying. Shakey Bee bottom lip all swole up with Sweet Peach and me explainin how come the sweet-potato bread was a dollar-quarter this time stead of dollar regular and he say uh hunh he understand, then he break into this *thizzin* kind of hum which is quiet, but fiercesome just the same, if you ain't ready for it. Which I wasn't. But I got used to it and the onliest time I had to say somethin bout it was when he was playin checkers on the stoop one time and he commenst to hummin quite churchy seem to me. So I says, 'Look here Shakey Bee, I can't beat you and Jesus too.' He stop.

So that's how come I asked My Man Bovanne to dance. He ain't my man mind you, just a nice ole gent from the block that we all know cause he fixes things and the kids like him. Or used to fore Black Power got hold their minds and mess em around till they can't be civil to ole folks. So we at this benefit for my niece's cousin who's runnin for somethin with this Black party somethin or other behind her. And I press up close to dance with Bovanne who blind and I'm hummin and he hummin, chest to chest like talkin. Not jammin my breasts into the man. Wasn't bout tits. Was bout vibrations. And he dug it and asked me what color dress I had on and how my hair was fixed and how I was doin without a man, not nosy but nice-like, and who was at this affair and was the canapés dainty-stingy or healthy enough to get hold of proper. Comfy and cheery is what I'm tryin to get across. Touch talkin like the heel of the hand on the tambourine or on a drum.

But right away Joe Lee come up on us and frown for dancin so close to the man. My own son who knows what kind of warm I am about; and don't grown men call me long distance and in the middle of the night for a little Mama comfort? But he frown. Which ain't right since Bovanne can't see and defend himself. Just a nice old man who fixes toasters and busted irons and bicycles and things and changes the lock on my door when my men friends get messy. Nice man. Which is not why they invited him. Grass roots you see. Me and Sister Taylor and the woman who does heads at Mamies and the man from the barber shop, we all there on account of we grass roots. And I ain't never been souther than Brooklyn Battery and no more country than the window box on my fire escape. And just yesterday my kids tellin me to take them countrified rags off my head and be cool. And now can't get Black enough to suit em. So everybody passin sayin My Man Bovanne. Big deal, keep steppin and don't even stop a minute to get the man a drink or one of them cute sandwiches or tell him what's going on. And him standin there with a smile ready case someone do speak he want to be ready. So that's how come I pull him on the dance floor and we dance squeezin past the tables and chairs and all them coats and people standin round up in each other face talkin bout this and that but got no use for this blind man who mostly fixed skates and skooters for all these folks when they was just kids. So I'm pressed up close and we touch talkin with the hum. And here come my daughter cuttin her eye at me like she do when she tell me about my 'apolitical' self like I got hoof and mouf disease and there ain't no hope at all. And I don't pay her no mind and just look up in Bovanne shadow face and tell him his stomach like a drum and he laugh. Laugh real loud. And here come my youngest, Task, with a tap on my elbow like he the third grade monitor and I'm cuttin up on the line to assembly.

'I was just talkin on the drums,' I explained when they hauled me into the kitchen. I figured drums was my best defense. They can get ready for drums what with all this heritage business. And Bovanne stomach just like that drum Task give me when he come back from Africa. You just touch it and it hum thizzm, thizzm. So I stuck to the drum story. 'Just drummin that's all.'

'Mama, what are you talkin about?'

'She had too much to drink,' say Elo to Task cause she don't hardly say nuthin to me direct no more since that ugly argument about my wigs.

'Look here Mama,' say Task, the gentle one. 'We just tryin to pull your coat. You were makin a spectacle of yourself out there dancing like that.'

'Dancin like what?'

Task run a hand over his left ear like his father for the world and his father before that.

'Like a bitch in heat,' say Elo.

'Well uhh, I was goin to say like one of them sex-starved ladies gettin on in years and not too discriminating. Know what I mean?'

I don't answer cause I'll cry. Terrible thing when your own children talk to you like that. Pullin me out the party and hustlin me into some stranger's kitchen in the back of a bar just like the damn police. And ain't like I'm old old. I can still wear me some sleeveless dresses without the meat hanging off my arm. And I keep up with some thangs through my kids. Who ain't kids no more. To hear them tell it. So I don't say nuthin.

'Dancin with that tom,' say Elo to Joe Lee, who leanin on the folks' freezer. 'His feet can smell a cracker a mile away and go into their shuffle number post haste. And them eyes. He could be a little considerate and put on some shades. Who wants to look into them blown-out fuses that –'

'Is this what they call the generation gap?' I say.

'Generation gap,' spits Elo, like I suggested castor oil and fricassee possum in the milk-shakes or somethin. 'That's a white concept for a white phenomenon. There's no generation gap among Black people. We are a col –'

'Yeh, well never mind,' says Joe Lee. 'The point is Mama ... well, it's pride. You embarrass yourself and us too dancin like that.'

'I wasn't shame.' Then nobody say nuthin. Them standin there in they pretty clothes with drinks in they hands and gangin up on me, and me in the third-degree chair and nary a olive to my name. Felt just like the police got hold to me.

'First of all,' Task say, holdin up his hand and tickin off the offenses, 'the dress. Now that dress is too short, Mama, and too low-cut for a woman your age. And Tamu's going to make a speech tonight to kick off the campaign and will be introducin you and expecting you to organize the council of elders –'

'Me? Didn nobody ask me nuthin. You mean Nisi? She change her name?'

'Well, Norton was supposed to tell you about it. Nisi wants to introduce you and then encourage the older folks to form a Council of the Elders to act as an advisory –'

'And you going to be standing there with your boobs out and that wig on your head and that hem up to your ass. And people'll say, "Ain't that the horny bitch that was grindin with the blind dude?"'

'Elo, be cool a minute,' say Task, gettin to the next finger. 'And then there's the drinkin. Mama, you know you can't drink cause next thing you know you be laughin loud and carryin on,' and he grab another finger for the loudness. 'And then there's the dancin. You been tattooed on the man for four records straight and slow draggin even on the fast numbers. How you think that look for a woman your age?'

'What's my age?'

'What?'

'I'm axin you all a simple question. You keep talkin bout what's proper for a woman my age. How old am I anyhow?' And Joe Lee slams his eyes shut and squinches up his face to figure. And Task run a hand over his ear and stare into his glass like the ice cubes goin calculate for him. And Elo just starin at the top of my head like she goin rip the wig off any minute now.

'Is your hair braided up under that thing? If so, why don't you take it off? You always did do a neat cornroll.'

'Uh huh,' cause I'm thinkin how she couldn't undo her hair fast enough talking bout cornroll so countrified. None of which was the subject. 'How old, I say?'

'Sixtee-one or –'

'You a damn lie Joe Lee Peoples.'

'And that's another thing,' say Task on the fingers.

'You know what you all can kiss,' I say, gettin up and brushin the wrinkles out my lap.

'Oh, Mama,' Elo say, puttin a hand on my shoulder like she hasn't done since she left home and the hand landin light and not sure it supposed to be there. Which hurt me to my heart. Cause this was the child in our happiness fore Mr Peoples die. And I carried that child strapped to my chest till she was nearly two. We close is what I'm tryin to tell you. Cause it was more me in the child than the others. And even after Task it was the girlchild I covered in the night and wept over for no reason at all less it was she was a chub-chub like me and not very pretty, but a warm child. And how did things get to this, that she can't put a sure hand on me and say Mama we love you and care about you and you entitled to enjoy yourself cause you a good woman?

'And then there's Reverend Trent,' say Task, glancin from left to right like they hatchin a plot and just now lettin me in on it. 'You were suppose to be talking with him tonight, Mama, about giving us his basement for campaign headquarters and –'

'Didn nobody tell me nuthin. If grass roots mean you kept in the dark I can't use it. I really can't. And Reven Trent a fool anyway the way he tore into the widow man up there on Edgecomb cause he wouldn't take in three of them foster children and the woman not even comfy in the ground yet and the man's mind messed up and –'

'Look here,' say Task. 'What we need is a family conference so we can get all this stuff cleared up and laid out on the table. In the meantime I think we better get back into the other room and tend to business. And in the meantime, Mama, see if you can't get to Reverend Trent and –'

'You want me to belly rub with the Reven, that it?'

'Oh damn,' Elo say and go through the swingin door.

'We'll talk about all this at dinner. How's tomorrow night, Joe Lee?' While Joe Lee being self-important I'm wonderin who's doin the cookin and how come no body ax me if I'm free and do I get a corsage and things like that. Then Joe nod that it's O.K. and he go through the swingin door and just a little hubbub come through from the other room. Then Task smile his smile, lookin just like his daddy and he leave. And it just me in this stranger's kitchen, which was a mess I wouldn't never let my kitchen look like. Poison you just to look at the pots. Then the door swing the other way and it's My Man Bovanne standin there sayin Miss Hazel but lookin at the deep fry and then at the steam table, and most surprised when I come up on him from the other direction and take him on out of there. Pass the folks pushin up towards the stage where Nisi and some other people settin and ready to talk,

and folks gettin to the last of the sandwiches and the booze fore they settle
down in one spot and listen serious. And I'm thinkin bout tellin Bovanne
what a lovely long dress Nisi got on and the earrings and her hair piled up in
a cone and the people bout to hear how we all gettin screwed and gotta form
our own party and everybody there listenin and lookin. But instead I just haul
the man on out of there, and Joe Lee and his wife look at me like I'm terrible,
but they ain't said boo to the man yet. Cause he blind and old and don't
nobody there need him since they grown up and don't need they skates fixed
no more.

'Where we goin, Miss Hazel?' Him knowin all the time.

'First we gonna buy you some dark sunglasses. Then you comin with me
to the supermarket so I can pick up tomorrow's dinner, which is goin to be a
grand thing proper and you invited. Then we goin to my house.'

'That be fine. I surely would like to rest my feet.' Bein cute, but you got to
let men play out they little show, blind or not. So he chat on bout how tired
he is and how he appreciate me takin him in hand this way. And I'm thinkin
I'll have him change the lock on my door first thing. Then I'll give the man a
nice warm bath with jasmine leaves in the water and a little Epsom salt on the
sponge to do his back. And then a good rubdown with rose water and olive
oil. Then a cup of lemon tea with a taste in it. And a little talcum, some of
that fancy stuff Nisi mother sent over last Christmas. And then a massage, a
good face massage round the forehead which is the worryin part. Cause you
gots to take care of the older folks. And let them know they still needed to
run the mimeo machine and keep the spark plugs clean and fix the mailboxes
for folks who might help us get the breakfast program goin, and the school
for the little kids and the campaign and all. Cause old folks is the nation.
That what Nisi was sayin and I mean to do my part.

'I imagine you are a very pretty woman, Miss Hazel.'

'I surely am,' I say just like the hussy my daughter always say I was.

- *How did you respond to this story?*
- *Toni Cade Bambara has commented that her interest in language is 'trying to break words open and get at the bones'. From your reading of this story, what do you think this means?*
- *'First you un-name yourself, then you reach back into your oppressed and bloody and exploited and magical history, and reclaim. Then you begin crafting out a new voice' (Bambara). On the evidence of* My Man Bovanne, *has the writer succeeded in the task of reclaiming an identity and of developing a distinct voice for black people?*

ACCENT AND DIALECT

- *Read the poems that follow. In small groups prepare a presentation of the poems either for a tape recording or for performance. Your presentation should include one or more alternative readings of each poem (for example in your own accent, in the designated accent, in Received Pronunciation).*

1   THE WIFE A-LOST

Since I noo mwore do zee your feace,
   Up steairs or down below,
I'll zit me in the lwonesome pleace,
   Where flat-bough'd beech do grow;
Below the beeches' bough, my love,
   Where you did never come,
An' I don't look to meet ye now,
   As I do look at hwome.

Since you noo mwore be at my zide,
   In walks in zummer het,
I'll goo alwone where mist do ride,
   Drough trees a-drippen wet;
Below the rain-wet bough my love,
   Where you did never come,
An I don't grieve to miss ye now,
   As I do grieve at hwome.

Since now bezide my dinner-bwoard
   Your vaice do never sound,
I'll eat the bit I can avvword,
   A-yield upon the ground;
Below the darksome bough, my love,
   Where you did never dine,
An' I don't grieve to miss ye now,
   As I at hwome do pine.

Since I do miss your vaice and feace
   In prayer at eventide,
I'll pray wi' woone sad vaice vor greace
   To goo where you do bide;
Above the tree an' bough, my love,
   Where you be gone avore,
An' be a-waiten vor me now,
   To come vor evermwore.

               William Barnes

2   FROM: UNRELATED INCIDENTS

(3)
this is thi
six a clock
news thi
man said n
thi reason
a talk wia
BBC accent
iz coz yi
widny wahnt
mi ti talk

aboot thi
trooth wia
voice lik
wanna yoo
scruff. if
a toktaboot
thi trooth
lik wanna yoo
scruff yi
widny thingk
it wuz troo.
jist wanna yoo
scruff tokn.
thirza right
wayti spell
ana right way
ti tok it, this
is me tokn yir
right way a
spellin. this
is ma trooth.
yooz doant no
thi trooth
yirsellz cawz
yi canny talk
right. this is
the six a clock
nyooz. belt up.

Tom Leonard

- *Account for any problems you might have encountered in producing a reading of the poems.*
- *How far does the impact of the poems lie in their performance?*
- *What do you think might be the advantages or disadvantages of writing poetry in dialect?*

When we consider accents and dialects we tend to assume there is a standard model of the language from which they deviate and that this model (the Queen's English, Standard English or Received Pronunciation) is a more correct and 'proper' form of English. However, language is always changing (think of Chaucer's or Shakespeare's English) and one form of it assumes superiority not because it is somehow more pure, but because of social factors such as the attitudes of the governing classes, the effect of the mass media and institutions like the education system. One could argue that Standard English is only another dialect, that of the southern middle or upper classes.

- *How close to Standard English is the language you use at home or with your friends? Would it be effective to communicate with someone from a different area, social class or racial background?*

- *In what ways do you think your views on the English language have been influenced by your own background?*

CLASS

Certain sections of society or certain races seem to have dominated literature as they have done with language, particularly what we tend to see as 'classic' literature. Some written forms of literature have a more 'exclusive' image than others. Poetry in particular tends to be considered the practice of the leisured upper and middle classes who can indulge in 'art for art's sake' and who know exactly how to handle the structures and metres of intricate forms like the sonnet.

What implications does this have for a poet from a working-class background? Many of Tony Harrison's poems are concerned with his Leeds working-class background and confront these issues.

- *Study the poems below and prepare a reading of them, perhaps using different voices in your performance.*

THEM & [UZ]

for Professors Richard Hoggart & Leon Cortez

I

αἰαῖ, ay, ay! . . . stutterer Demosthenes
gob full of pebbles outshouting seas –

4 words only of *mi 'art aches* and . . . 'Mine's broken,
you barbarian, T. W.!' *He* was nicely spoken.
'Can't have our glorious heritage done to death!'

I played the Drunken Porter in *Macbeth*.

'Poetry's the speech of kings. You're one of those
Shakespeare gives the comic bits to: prose!
All poetry (even Cockney Keats?) you see
's been dubbed by [ʌs] into RP,
Received Pronunciation, please believe [ʌs]
your speech is in the hands of the Receivers.'

'We say [ʌs] not [uz], T. W.!' That shut my trap.
I doffed my flat a's (as in 'flat cap')
my mouth all stuffed with glottals, great
lumps to hawk up and spit out . . . *E-nun-ci-ate*!

II

So right, yer buggers, then! We'll occupy
your lousy leasehold Poetry.

I chewed up Littererchewer and spat the bones
into the lap of dozing Daniel Jones,
dropped the initials I'd been harried as
and used my *name* and own voice: [uz] [uz] [uz],
ended sentences with by, with, from,
and spoke the language that I spoke at home.
RIP RP, RIP T. W.
I'm *Tony* Harrison no longer you!

You can tell the Receivers where to go
(and not aspirate it) once you know
Wordsworth's *matter/water* are full rhymes,
[uz] can be loving as well as funny.

My first mention in the *Times*
automatically made Tony Anthony!

Tony Harrison

THE QUEEN'S ENGLISH

Last meal together, Leeds, the Queen's Hotel,
that grandish pile of swank in City Square.
Too posh for me! he said (though he dressed well)
If you weren't wi' me now ah'd nivver dare!

I knew that he'd decided that he'd die
not by the way he lingered in the bar,
nor by that look he'd give with one good eye,
nor the firmer handshake and the gruff *ta-ra*,
but when we browsed the station bookstall sales
he picked up *Poems from the Yorkshire Dales* –

'ere tek this un wi' yer to New York
to remind yer 'ow us gaffers used to talk.
It's up your street in't it? ah'll buy yer that!

The broken lines go through me speeding South –

As t'Doctor stopped to oppen woodland yat . . .
and
    wi' skill they putten wuds reet i' his mouth.

Tony Harrison

- *What difficulties, if any, did you encounter in reading the poems?*
- *What do the poems suggest about the relationship of the poet to social class?*
- *In what ways is language presented as an aspect of this relationship?*
- *In what ways do these poems appear to you to be traditional or innovative?*
- *One of the striking features of Harrison's sonnets, for example in 'The Queen's English', is the way they use different voices and languages within the form of the poem. Try writing your own poem which makes use of the quoted voice to highlight a contrast of language, for example, vernacular/ standard, regional/race, child/adult, teacher/pupil.*

Reading List

For examples of fiction from black American writers try:
Gorilla, My Love, Toni Cade Bambara (The Women's Press, 1984)
The Color Purple, Alice Walker (The Women's Press, 1983)
Beloved, Toni Morrison (Chatto and Windus, 1987)

There are many black poets now finding a voice. Try Linton Kwesi
Johnson, Grace Nichols, John Agard, James Berry, Amryl Johnson.
Anthologies are a good place to start. *The Penguin Book of Caribbean
Verse in English* edited by Paula Burnett (Penguin, 1986) spans the 'oral'
and 'literary' tradition from eighteenth century to contemporary poets.
News for Babylon edited by James Berry (Chatto and Windus, 1984) is
another stimulating anthology.

Twelve More Modern Scottish Poets edited by Charles King and Iain
Crichton Smith (Hodder and Stoughton, 1986) features a number of
dialect poets.

THE GENDERED VOICE

THE PRESENTATION OF WOMEN

Consider the presentation of women in each of the following extracts.

1

1 We are having supper.
Daddy has just come in from work.

2 Mummy buys our food
at a supermarket.
She is buying bread, meat
and cheese.

3 Some food must be cooked.
Other kinds of food
do not need cooking.
Salad is not cooked.

(from a book in a reading scheme for young children)

2 'But I don't want to . . .' began Berta, and then felt a firm hand on her arm. It was Julian.

'Come on, kid,' he said. 'Be your age! Remember you're a guest here and put on a few of your best manners. We like American children – but not *spoilt* ones!'

Berta had quite a shock to hear Julian speaking like this. She looked up at him and he grinned down at her. She felt near tears, but she smiled back.

'You haven't any brothers to keep you in your place,' said Julian, linking his arm in hers. 'Well, from now on, while you're here, Dick and I are your brothers, and you've got to toe the line, just like Anne. See? What about it?'

Berta felt that there was nothing in the world she would like better than having Julian for a brother! He was big and tall and had twinkling kindly eyes that made Berta feel he was as responsible and trustable as her father.

Aunt Fanny smiled to herself. Julian always knew the best thing to say and do. Now he would take Berta in hand and see she didn't upset the household too much. She was glad. It wasn't easy to run a big family like this, with a scientist husband to cope with, unless everyone pulled together!

'You go and help Aunt Fanny with the beds,' said Julian to Berta . . .

(from *Five have Plenty of Fun*, a children's novel by Enid Blyton)

3   'I came up,' he said, speaking curiously matter-of-fact and level, 'to ask if you'd marry me. You are free, aren't you?' . . . She quivered, feeling herself created, will-less, lapsing into him, into a common will with him.

'You want me?' she said.

A pallor came over his face.

'Yes,' he said.

Still there was suspense and silence.

'No,' she said, not of herself. 'No, I don't know.'

He felt the tension breaking up in him, his fists slackened, he was unable to move. He stood looking at her, helpless in his vague collapse. For the moment she had become unreal to him. Then he saw her come to him, curiously direct and as if without movement, in a sudden flow. She put her hand to his coat.

'Yes, I want to,' she said, impersonally, looking at him with wide, candid, newly-opened eyes, opened now with supreme truth. He went very white as he stood, and did not move, only his eyes were held by hers, and he suffered. She seemed to see him with her newly-opened, wide eyes, almost of a child, and with a strange movement, that was agony to him, she reached slowly forward her dark face and her breast to him, with a slow insinuation of a kiss that made something break in his brain, and it was darkness over him for a few moments.

He had her in his arms, and, obliterated, was kissing her. And it was sheer, blenched agony to him, to break away from himself. She was there so small and light and accepting in his arms, like a child . . .

(from *The Rainbow*, a novel by D. H. Lawrence)

4   PRE-NATAL TESTS

Throughout pregnancy, checks are made on the pregnant woman to make sure that she and her baby are progressing normally. Among these are weight tests, uterus size, blood pressure, blood tests, urine tests and amniocentesis.

Every time the pregnant mother visits the ante-natal clinic she will be weighed. She will be expected to show a weight gain of about a half a kilogram a week in the latter half of pregnancy, but excessive weight gain is a problem. This is because excessive weight gain may indicate the retention of abnormal amounts of fluid by the mother. This is called oedema and may lead to high blood pressure and kidney problems, and in severe cases to a disease called eclampsia when the high blood pressure causes convulsions . . .

> (from *Human Biology* by Rowlinson and Jenkins, a textbook for secondary
> school students)

5   Man is distinguished from other animals by his imaginative gifts. He makes plans, inventions, new discoveries, by putting different talents together; and his discoveries become more subtle and penetrating, as he learns to combine his talents in more complex and intimate ways. So the great discoveries of different ages and different cultures, in technique, in science, in the arts, express in their progression a richer and more intricate conjunction of human faculties, an ascending trellis of his gifts.

> (from *The Ascent of Man* by Jacob Bronowski, a book accompanying a
> television series)

6
>
> Ye tradefull Merchants, that with weary toyle,
>   do seeke most pretious things to make your gain;
> and both the Indias of their treasures spoile,
>   what needeth you to seeke so farre in vaine?
> For loe my love doth in her selfe containe
>   all this worlds riches that may farre be found,
> if Saphyres, loe her eies be Saphyres plaine,
>   if Rubies, loe her lips be Rubies sound:
> If pearles, hir teeth be pearles both pure and round;
>   if Yvorie, her forhead yvory weene;
> if silver, her faire hands are silver sheene.
> But that which fairest is, but few behold,
>   her mind adorned with vertues manifold.

> (from *Amoretti* by Edmund Spenser, an Elizabethan poet)

- *Discuss the roles played by women in each of the extracts.*
- *Through whose eyes do we view the women and what attitudes are we expected to share?*
- *What assumptions does each extract make about*
  a) *women?*
  b) *men?*
  c) *readers?*
- *Examine the type of language which is used to speak of the female gender. Pay particular attention to the vocabulary, imagery and tone.*

Literature is an important means whereby prevailing attitudes towards women are both reflected and perpetuated. Even before we attend our first English Literature class, we have become used to literature which speaks of women in particular ways.

THE GENDERED VOICE

Read the following extracts from novels:

1   She wanders disconsolately between the bathroom and the kitchen, putting the kettle on, sucking her pepperminty toothbrush, pondering, trying to hang on to her dream, coaxing it to stay and reveal itself. But it slips past her; it vanishes before she can catch at its trailing ribbons. Like the moon, it slips inexorably away, to be replaced by the solid shapes of things seen by daylight.

These include the wooden table she carries on to the balcony from the kitchen, the black cast-iron frying-pan, sizzling with tender pink bacon and the white flaps of eggs, the glossy yellow crocuses blooming at the foot of the apple tree. Helen settles herself on the wooden chair she has drawn up at the table, and is overcome by the smells and tastes of breakfast eaten outside. Hot coffee steam curls up in the sunlight, and there is hot sun on her face and on the piece of brown toast she holds in her hand. The bread is nutty and rich, a pleasure to chew and swallow, with a hint of molasses lingering afterwards on her tongue. Robert tasted sharp and salty. He is not here to taste the breakfast picnic, to see the light dancing through the glass of the marmalade jar on the strong, bitter strands of orange. She rolls her tongue around her mouth, going over in her memory all the moments of the night, and then abandoning them for the pleasures of the present.

This is her favourite place to sit. The distinction between outside and inside the house is blurred. She is still of the house, and almost of the garden, yet belonging totally to neither. She shares the privacy and the enclosure of the house with the openness and vegetation of the garden; she is the point at which they meet and overlap. She faces out, looking through the wrought-iron tracery of the balcony over the big garden beginning a few feet below her, at the crescent of the houses opposite forming her boundary on the other side.

Above her, very much defining her garden room, rears a fifty-foot weeping ash. It grows to the right of her, its trunk bent near its base so that the great mass of the tree drops to the left, its topmost branches reaching as high as the roof, waving graceful fronds to blind all the windows with green, and its lower branches drooping to form an umbrella-shaped tent between her and the garden. Joining house and garden in this way, acting as entrance pavilion and as resting-place, the tree has a special charm added to that of its size and height, its long slender leaves, its delicate constant movements, its shape.

2   'Come along, there. Come along,' cried Mrs Hardcastle, petulantly, as she lit the candle: 'Harry. Sal. . . . D'y' hear?' She shook one of the forms.

A smothered grumbling. Sally withdrew her head from the thin coverings and yawned. Eighteen, a gorgeous creature whose native beauty her shabbiness could not hide. Eyes dark, lustrous, haunting; abundant black hair tumbling in waves; a full, ripe, pouting mouth and a low, round bosom. A face and form such as any society dame would have given three-quarters of her fortune to possess. Sally wore it carelessly as though youth's brief hour was eternal; as though there was no such thing as old age. She failed in her temper; but when roused, colour tinted her pallid cheeks such as the wind whipped up when it blew from the north or east.

'Tea brewed, ma?' she asked, rubbing her eyes.

'Long since,' her mother lied, adding, plaintively: 'Come on wi' y'. Get up. ... Havin' me trapesin' about like this. ... Why can't y' get up first call. ... When I was your age I was up wi' t' lark. ... Harry. *Harry.* Y'll be late for work. Oh, *willy'* get up. Sick an' tired I am wastin' breath.'

Sally prodded him with her elbow: 'Hey, dopey ... D'y hear ...? Gerrup.' ...

Sally said, after she had washed herself: 'What's up wi' *you* this morning Why are y' rushin' wi' y' breakfast; y've plenty o' time.'

She *would* say that. 'You mind y'r own business,' he muttered.

She smiled as she glanced at his rolled-up sleeves: 'Old Samson,' she said, with a provocative laugh: 'All muscle.'

He flushed hotly: this was her favourite trick, deriding his miserable muscles when she couldn't think of anything else to say; had been ever since once she had surprised him, stripped to the waist, standing in front of the small mirror over the slopstone endeavouring to emulate the posture of a notorious wrestler whose picture had lain propped against a jug on the table: it had been, for him, a most embarrassing moment. 'You leave my arms alone,' he snapped. He raised his brows accusingly: 'You watch yourself. Ah saw y' talkin' t' Ned Narkey, last night. What time did he let y' come in, eh? That's what Ah'd like t' know. If pa hears about –'

Her eyes blazed; the smile faded: 'You mind your own business,' contemptuously, and with a curl of the lip: 'Choir boy! Ha!'

- *What do you think is the gender of the writer of each passage? (You will find the answers at the end of this chapter.)*
- *What factors did you consider in seeking an answer?*
- *One of these writers is attempting to write in a 'gendered voice': i.e. the structure and expression of the prose is intended to convey the unique experience of the female psyche. Which passage do you think is written in a 'gendered voice' and how do you identify it? Do you think it is a good idea to create a 'gendered voice'? Do you think it is possible?*

WOMEN AND LANGUAGE

A riddle:

A man and his son are injured in a car accident. The man dies, but the boy is rushed to the nearest hospital. As he is wheeled into the emergency treatment room, the doctor glances at his face and cries out: 'That's my son!'

- *What is the relationship between the doctor and the patient?*

The explanation is simple: the doctor is the boy's mother. We just don't expect a woman doctor. Another exercise: consider the distinctions which have developed between these words with the same origin: *master/mistress, governor/governess, hero/heroine, dog/bitch, bachelor/spinster.*

- *What different implications are there between the 'male' and 'female' words in each case?*
- *Can you think of other words which are 'gender-loaded'?*

Men's work has given them the skills to use language in a wide range of situations – the board room, the office, the pub, the home, the factory floor. Women writers have traditionally belonged to the higher classes who were taught to read and write, but whose experience was confined to domestic life. There they developed a language for intimate and domestic circumstances, but received little preparation for public or vocational roles. Though it may be dismissed as 'gossip', women are commonly thought to talk more freely than men about their everyday experiences, their relationships and feelings.

- *Clearly, women are at a disadvantage in their careers if they cannot master the public voice. But are there ways in which men are deprived if they cannot talk intimately?*

The language used in 'high places' is part of the male world. Think for example of the kind of language used by platform speakers, official forms, political leaders, commerce, law or even by the great poets of the past. These are forms of language which have been developed and dominated by men. Women who do establish careers in these areas of public life learn the language but pay a price: they are labelled 'unfeminine', 'strident' or 'bossy'.

- *Think of prominent women, such as Margaret Thatcher, who have achieved public office and discuss your impressions of their public-speaking styles.*

Women writers who wish to record their experience have to work with language, forms and conventions which have been developed by and for men. Women sometimes feel they have to be 'thieves of language' taking on vocabularies and forms which are more suited to the male experience. Traditionally women writers have favoured forms such as letters, diaries or even romantic novels which are considered to have a lower status than those like the epic, traditionally written by men.

- *Can you account for this difference in the type of literary form favoured by male and female writers?*

Several writers – whose names you will find at the end of the chapter – are trying to reclaim literature for women, to speak of experiences which cannot be conveyed by traditional 'male' language. Indeed, many recent poems by women address this very problem – the way language snares meaning.

Here are two examples – poems by Michele Roberts – which

manipulate conventional language to make the reader conscious of the problem.

- *Read the poems, and discuss the way their language prompts the reader to review sexist attitudes:*

'WOMEN'S ENTRY INTO CULTURE IS EXPERIENCED AS A LACK'

he wishes he were a
one of those able to
dance and shake
breasts and belly and hips
loose, a
not-himself, nothing-but

he wishes they did not have a
hiding from it in his bed stillness
he bruises easily

he wishes he were still a little boy
so that he did not have to face them
telling him he is an oppressor
he needs them to scold him
darling oppressor

if he were a
he would join the   movement
but at least his   friends
are always   who struggle

he has nothing to do but
help them out of
silence, he has
nothing else to do
with   oppression

he wishes they had a   too
so they could all just be friends

Michele Roberts

MIDDLE-CLASS HERO

he keeps himself inside a
no, sorry, he's a
no, that's it, *yes*:
he's got a

stereo
a motorbike, a library
a pair of jeans, and so
he's not into things
he can't relate
to who women are

they just cross
and tangle
his mind

he lustens to the rodeo, the sweet
mewsic of his own
spheres, he tames motorbooks
ejokulates the Word
into chamberpets, and wears
his blue meanies
with a tight
lip

he can't relate
to women who are

Michele Roberts

- *Do you think men and women speak in different ways, and if so, can you
  give examples? Consider your own use of language. Would a written
  transcript of your speech be easily identified as that of a man or a woman?*
- *Have there been occasions when you felt that you had to speak or behave in
  a particular way because of your gender? Were you ever told or shown how
  to behave like a boy or a girl? Prepare a poem or a short essay drawing on
  these experiences.*

WOMEN AS WRITERS

. . . any woman born with a great gift in the sixteenth century would certainly
have gone crazed, shot herself, or ended her days in some lonely cottage
outside the village, half-witch, half-wizard, feared and mocked at.

Virginia Woolf

So there hasn't been a female Shakespeare. Three possible answers: (a) So
what (this is simplest and best). (b) There hasn't been a *male* Shakespeare
since Shakespeare, dammit. (c) Somewhere, Franz Fanon opines that one
cannot, in reason, ask a shoeless peasant in the Upper Volta to write songs
like Schubert's; the opportunity to do so has never existed. The concept is
meaningless.

Angela Carter

- *How many famous women writers can you name? Some novelists, certainly
  – what about poets and playwrights?*
- *Why are there so few women writers compared to men?*

Virginia Woolf said 'a woman must have money and a room of her
own if she is to write fiction'. Until this century she also needed to be
educated, probably unmarried and childless, or at least able to restrict

her pregnancies and have domestic help. Even then, writing was often a secretive activity squeezed in around domestic duties. Jane Austen wrote her novels on a small table in the living room listening for the creak of the door hinge and hiding her work under blotting paper as people came in; Elizabeth Gaskell wrote amidst constant household interruptions and children. So being an invalid like Elizabeth Barrett was actually quite useful, ensuring time and privacy to write. Today's writer in comparison may feel, like Angela Carter, 'a new kind of being' with more freedom from such problems, but to write it is also necessary to feel confidence in your ability and entitlement to do so and to break into a world of rules, forms and traditions presided over by men.

Even the most highly rated authors, such as the Brontë sisters or George Eliot, adopted male pseudonyms to gain admission to the public world of writing. These writers are well-known now but they are a small group who got round the difficulties of being published, accepted and passed on to the next generation: many books by women popular in their time have vanished. In recent years, women's publishing groups such as Virago and The Women's Press have sought to retrieve this lost history of women's writing and to support the publication of contemporary writers.

ATTITUDES TO WRITING

One woman who succeeded in 'qualifying' as a poet was Elizabeth Barrett who married Robert Browning, also a poet. She was perhaps the more popular and admired writer before they married (he introduced himself through a fan letter) but today he is more widely known and read. In the following letters written before their marriage, Robert comments on the 'duty' of writing and invites Elizabeth's response. Her reply suggests the vulnerability she feels as a writer:

Robert to Elizabeth:

> You must read books in order to get words and forms for 'the public' if you write, and that you needs must do, if you fear God. I have no pleasure in writing myself – none, in the mere act – though all pleasure in the sense of fulfilling a duty, whence if I have done my real best, judge how heartbreaking a matter must it be to be pronounced a poor creature by critic this and acquaintance the other! But I think you like the operation of writing as I should like that of painting or making music, do you not?

Elizabeth to Robert:

> What you say of society draws me to many comparative thoughts of your life and mine. You seem to have drunken of the cup of life full, with the sun shining on it. I have lived only inwardly; or with sorrow, for a strong emotion.

Before this seclusion of my illness, I was secluded still, and there are few of
the youngest women in the world who have not seen more, heard more,
known more, of society, than I, who am scarcely to be called young now . . .

And do you also know what a disadvantage this ignorance is to my art?
Why, if I live on and yet do not escape from this seclusion, do you not
perceive that I labour under signal disadvantages – that I am, in a manner, a
blind poet? Certainly, there is a compensation to a degree. I have had much
of the inner life, and from the habit of self-consciousness and self-analysis, I
make great guesses at Human nature in the main. But how willingly I would
as a poet exchange some of this lumbering, ponderous, helpless knowledge
of books, for some experience of life and man . . .

I have lived all my chief joys, and indeed nearly all emotions that go
warmly by that name and relate to myself personally, in poetry and poetry
alone. Like to write? Of course, of course I do. I seem to live while I write – it
is life, for me . . . Is it not so with you? – oh, it must be so! For the rest, there
will be necessarily a reaction; and in my own particular case, whenever I see
a poem of mine in print, or even smoothly transcribed, the reaction is most
painful. The pleasure, the sense of power, without which I could not write a
line, is gone in a moment; and nothing remains but disappointment and
humiliation. I never wrote a poem which you could not persuade me to tear
to pieces if you took me at the right moment!

- *Compare the attitude of the two poets towards their writing.*
- *In the light of this discussion, what do you find interesting in this poem by
  Elizabeth Barrett Browning?*

> And will thou have me fashion into speech
> The love I bear thee, finding words enough,
> And hold the torch out, while the winds are rough,
> Between our faces, to cast light on each? –
> I drop it at thy feet. I cannot teach
> My hand to hold my spirit so far off
> From myself – me – that I should bring thee proof
> In words, of love hid in me out of reach.
> Nay, let the silence of my womanhood
> Commend my woman-love to thy belief, –
> Seeing that I stand unwon, however wooed,
> And rend the garment of my life, in brief,
> By a most dauntless, voiceless fortitude,
> Lest one touch of this heart convey its grief.

THE WOMEN'S GHETTO

Many critics think it counter-productive to consider the writing of
women separately from that of men. They argue that it is condescend-
ing and that it tends to put women writers in a ghetto. Feminists argue
that women need deliberate encouragement and support to break into
publishing.

● *What are your views on the following news item which describes a publishing controversy in 1987?*

The feminist publishing house Virago has been taken for a painful and embarrassing ride over *Down the Road Worlds Away*, a set of stories by Rahila Khan about the cultural confusion of Asian girls growing up in white Britain. Virago was told the author was a shy and reclusive woman, and so accepted the book and published it last month without ever meeting her. Yesterday, however, they learnt through a literary agent exactly why Khan keeps herself to herself – she is a man, and a white one at that. Virago refused to give the author's real identity last night, and is busy trying to get nearly 10,000 books back from shops. 'It's not unknown in feminist publishing for men to pass themselves off as women,' said a Virago spokeswoman. 'But this is rather bizarre – the book was published for the Asian community and purported to represent the Asian community, and we feel particularly distressed for them.' The book was well-reviewed – it has 'hard-eyed realism', according to Virago's own blurb – and the BBC has also broadcast six of Khan's stories in the belief that she is an Asian woman.

The issues raised in this chapter are concerned with gender and are not simply a 'woman's problem': it is important to turn our attention to the way men too are represented in all the texts we encounter.

● *Select a range of extracts (similar to that of the opening exercise in this section) which depict men and boys. Consider how they construct attitudes and images of masculinity.*

Reading List

Women's publishing groups such as Virago and The Women's Press offer a wide range of publications.

Lives of Girls and Women
There are many autobiographical accounts of growing up such as:
I know Why the Caged Bird Sings, Maya Angelou (Virago, 1984)
Testament of Youth, Vera Brittain (Virago, 1978).
The theme of girls growing into women is a vast area of interest in women's fiction. The following centre on young women:
The Magic Toyshop, Angela Carter (Virago, 1981)
The Beggar Maid, Alice Munro (Penguin, 1981)
Invitation to the Waltz, Rosamund Lehman (Virago, 1981)

Women and Madness
Madness is a state which occurs again and again in novels by women: it is a way of expressing the frenzy and frustration of oppression, and poses interesting problems for the writer in communicating the breakdown of conventional logic. We have enjoyed:
The Yellow Wallpaper, Charlotte Perkins-Gilman (Virago, 1981)

The Bell Jar, Sylvia Plath (Faber and Faber, 1967)
The Ha Ha, Jennifer Dawson (Virago, 1985)
Beyond the Glass, Antonia White (Virago, 1979)
Wide Sargasso Sea, Jean Rhys (Penguin, 1987)
Surfacing, Margaret Atwood (Virago, 1979)

Poetry
Women are under-represented in poetry anthologies, particularly those
who wrote before this century. It's amazing to think that Elizabeth I was
an accomplished poet: historians have preferred to emphasise her
rivalries and court affairs.
    There are a handful of anthologies which attempt to redress the
balance:
The World Split Open, (ed.) Louise Bernikow (Women's Press, 1979)
Bread and Roses, (ed.) Diana Scott (Virago, 1982)
Scars Upon My Heart: women's poetry and verse of the first world war, (ed.)
Catherine Reilly (Virago, 1981)
In the Pink, (ed.) Raving Beauties (Women's Press, 1983)
The Penguin Book of Women Poets

Plays
There is a growing number of women dramatists working for stage,
television and film. Methuen have published several volumes in a series
called *Plays by Women*, each of which features a selection of writers.

Short Stories
Many women writers have been attracted to this form. Try an anthology
like *The Secret Self* edited by H. Lee (Dent, 1985) or *The Seven Deadly
Sins* edited by A. Fell (Serpent's Tail, 1988). Women short story writers
like Katherine Mansfield, Doris Lessing, Alice Munro and Angela
Carter are well established. We enjoyed Margaret Atwood's collection
Bluebeard's Egg (Jonathan Cape, 1987).

Criticism
There are many books now that consider the relationship of women to
literature. Some lively discussions include:
A Room of One's Own, Virginia Woolf (Chatto and Windus, 1984)
Letters to Alice, Fay Weldon (Hodder and Stoughton, 1985)
On Gender and Writing, (ed.) M. Wandor (Pandora Press, 1983)
Feminist Literary Theory, (ed.) M. Eagleton (Basil Blackwell, 1986)

Writers in 'The Gendered Voice'
1 comes from *The Visitation* by Michele Roberts.
2 is from *Love on the Dole* by Walter Greenwood.

COMPOSING THE SELF

CREATING MEMORIES

This is the second volume of my unreliable memoirs. For a palpable fantasy, the first volume was well enough received. It purported to be the true story of how the author grew from infancy through adolescence to early manhood, this sequence of amazing biological developments largely taking place in Kogarah, a suburb of Sydney, NSW, Australia. And indeed it *was* a true story, in the sense that I wasn't brought up in a Tibetan monastery or a castle on the Danube. The central character was something like my real self. If the characters around him were composites, they were obviously so, and with some justification. The friend who helps you dig tunnels in your back yard is rarely the same friend who ruins your summer by flying a model aeroplane into your mother's prize trifle, but a book with everybody in it would last as long as life, and never live at all.

(Clive James in the Preface to *Falling Towards England*)

- *Write a short autobiographical piece. Try to recreate for a small group of friends the experience and significance of the events to which you refer.*
- *Read your work aloud to each other in a group and note your feelings about doing so.*
- *What did you leave out and why? Would you change your account for a different audience, such as your parents?*
- *Identify those moments in your work which are well captured and those which seem less truthful. What is it about them which satisfies or dissatisfies you?*
- *Has writing about your experiences had any effect on your memory of those experiences?*

It is tempting to think of memory as a recorder which stores up all our experiences. Yet research suggests that memory is selective and we are busy shaping it even as events happen to us. We cannot re-experience our lives as if for the first time. We are caught up in a permanent 'now'. But in autobiography we can map the past, exploring and savouring its significant aspects.

THE IMAGINARY 'I'

Language is by nature orderly. Words, sentences and syntax impose a certain amount of control over the experiences described in them. But minute-by-minute experience is shapeless, the mind responding to the events of the moment in a variety of ways. What then, are the difficulties for a writer trying to convey the experience of the individual mind? Read and discuss this extract in which we listen in to the inner monologue of Molly Bloom as she dozes:

> the day I got him to propose to me yes first I gave him the bit of seedcake out of my mouth and it was leapyear like now yes 16 years ago my God after that long kiss I near lost my breath yes he said I was a flower of the mountain yes so we are flowers all a womans body yes that was one true thing he said in his life and the sun shines for you today yes that was why I liked him because I saw he understood or felt what a woman is and I knew I could always get round him and I gave him all the pleasure I could leading him on till he asked me to say yes and I wouldnt answer first only looked out over the sea and the sky I was thinking of so many things he didnt know of Mulvey and Mr Stanhope and Hester and father and old captain Groves [. . .] and O that awful deep-down torrent O and the sea the sea crimson sometimes like fire and the glorious sunsets and the figtrees in the Alameda gardens yes and all the queer little streets and pink and blue and yellow houses and the rosegardens and the jessamine and geraniums and cactuses and Gibraltar as a girl where I was a Flower of the mountain yes when I put the rose in my hair like the Andalusian girls used or shall I wear a red yes and how he kissed me under the Moorish wall and I thought well as well him as another and then I asked him with my eyes to ask again yes and then he asked me would I yes to say yes my mountain flower and first I put my arms around him yes and drew him down to me so he could feel my breasts all perfume yes and his heart was going like mad and yes I said yes I will Yes.

> (from *Ulysses* by James Joyce)

- *How has James Joyce tried to suggest the texture of thought?*
- *What insights does this narrative approach give us into the character of Molly Bloom?*
- *Listen in to your own 'stream of consciousness'. Some people hear a steady babble of words inside their heads, whilst others have images or something less definite than either of these things. Try describing or even recording your own inner monologue.*

It is very likely that your moment-by-moment experience is a jumble of sensations and impressions which you sort through and make sense of. Like most people, you probably continue to reflect on those aspects of experience which are interesting or significant for you. If you write your experience down, you may well select these aspects and present them to your reader in a descriptive or explanatory way. The result will probably represent the experience as more orderly than it actually was.

Because writing processes experience into a more controlled form, it can imply that one's perceptions, and therefore one's personality, are more controlled and coherent than is actually the case. The word 'I', for example, does not suggest the variety of faces we keep in life: daughter, sister, student, employee, friend. We adopt a different way of behaving in each case. The word 'I' assumes that at heart each one of us has a real self. How often have you been told to just 'be yourself' or to 'act naturally'? Does anyone have this true self at their core?

AUTOBIOGRAPHY AS FICTION

Here are several extracts – some are taken from autobiographies, others from novels and stories. Can you identify which are which?

1   I have no memory of majesty to match that one from Rotten Row. Even when the Twins Fred and Joe, who dealt so deviously in scrap at the other end of the alley near the wooden gate, were fetched away by two giraffe-like policemen the drama dwindled down into defeat. We watched one of the coppers walking, rolling up the alley and we muttered, I not knowing why. We watched Fred and Joe dash out of their house and bundle themselves through the wooden gate; but of course the second copper was standing on the other side. They ran right into him, small men, easily grabbed in either hand. They were brought down the alley handcuffed between two dark blue pillars surmounted by silver spikes, the van was waiting for them. We shouted and muttered and made the dull tearing sound that was Rotten Row's equivalent of booing. Fred and Joe were pale but perky. The coppers came, took, went, unstoppable as birth and death, the three cases in which Rotten Row accepted unconditional defeat. Whether the extra mouth was coming, or the policeman's van, or the long hearse that would draw up at the end of the passage, made no difference. A hand of some sort was thrust through the Row to take what it would and no one could stop it.

We were a world inside a world and I was a man before I achieved the intellectual revolution of thinking of us as a slum. Though we were only forty yards long and the fields lapped against us we were a slum. Most people think of slums as miles of muck in the East End of London or the jerry-built lean-to's of the Black Country. But we lived right in the heart of the Garden of England and the hop gardens glowed round us.

2   The kitchen was really quite small with a little window which looked out into the garden but which was so full of geraniums and wandering sailor that you could hardly see out. There was a range with a brass tap and knobs on the

oven doors, a big table where we all ate, beside the staircase, and a small cross-legged bamboo table where Mr Jane ate alone by the fire. He was very deaf and didn't like having to make conversation. He hardly ever spoke at all, actually. Sometimes he said in a very rumbling voice, 'Thank you, Mother,' or 'I think I'll be going up then,' or sometimes when he found something interesting in the local paper he'd say, 'I see they're at it again.' But you never knew who they were or what they were up to. So you couldn't answer him even to be polite. No one ever seemed to talk to him really. But, sometimes, when we were in bed, we could hear Mrs Jane's voice telling him what we had all been doing during the day. We never heard him, only her, because she had to talk very loudly. Their room was next door to ours so we were able to hear everything pretty clearly. I felt rather uncomfortable and tried to make coughing noises so that she'd perhaps hear that we were awake. But she never did, and after a while I didn't bother any longer.

3   I was born in 1944, although I was imagined and planned long before that. My mother and father married in 1937, at the ages of thirty-four and thirty respectively. She came from a solid middle-class family in South London; her father, Thomas Miller, had a relatively prestigious job as a cutlery salesman. The house in which she grew up and to which I was taken as a child was itself impeccably respectable. The rooms were dark and smelt of polish and the paint was brown. A lace mat occupied the centre of the dining table, and on it stood a green glass bowl containing a china goldfish; tea was served in delicate white cups and good manners were expected. Thomas Miller's mother was the daughter of a Scottish sea captain and she grew up, shoeless, on the island of Rum, so my mother's background was a little more chequered than it appeared. Her own mother, Katie Louisa Miller, Thomas's wife, was the daughter of a Norfolk wheelwright and an Irish woman with a fiery temper, a combination that produced a woman with a dainty, mild-mannered appearance concealing a will of iron. 'Gran', as I knew her, wore stiff white blouses with round cameo brooches at the neck. She had a prim mouth, and only her luminous dark eyes gave one a glimpse of the unbuttoned person inside.

4   Laughing, they come into the room. Two beds, of which they will only occupy one: a lamp already streaking its pale light over jumbled papers. A cool, kind night outside, in which they found a restaurant with red-checked tables, flowers, flute music and a glowing spit, and nobody in it but themselves. They drank champagne and tried not to think about the future.

   They take off their clothes and lie on the bed. She is exhausted with going to bed, her own bed, late, and getting up early to see her daughter before joining him again. In fact, what with the lack of sleep and the champagne and a bout of crying earlier in a pub at the futility of it all, she cannot remember ever feeling so tired before. He is resolute in the face of her tiredness. This is their last chance this time to lie together like this, and who knows if there'll be another? He loves her, an amazing enough fact on its own, for love is a concept that does not come easily to him. He is going to make the best of the situation, adopting a pragmatic male attitude which is designed to cover up the real profundity of his feelings about this mess into which they have got themselves – or, rather, it could be said, into which he has got them.

5   I was found on the morning of December 31st on the steps of a Children's Home, near Oxford, on the Abingdon road. I was securely and warmly wrapped against the intense cold in four shawls and lay in a small wickerwork basket of the type commonly used for putting wood in. To the top shawl was pinned a note saying my name was Penelope and would someone please take care of me. Nothing else. No other evidence of maternal care or tenderness. I weighed only five and a half pounds but was in good health. It was quickly established that I was no more than four or five days old and that I was probably born prematurely (there were little flecks of a creamy-like substance in the folds of my skin, a sure sign). The cord was still attached to my navel, two inches of that rapidly withering tissue which had held me to my mother, but it had been expertly cut and tied, suggesting that the services of a midwife or other medical person had been employed.

In those days, it was difficult to trace the mother of an abandoned baby. Nobody took my photograph and printed it in a newspaper. The local hospitals were not subjected to close scrutiny nor were doctors and district nurses closely questioned about recent confinements in the area. Some forty years later, when I set about trying to trace my birth, I found no written record of any inquiries at all, and, naturally, neither the shawls nor the basket nor, more importantly, the note survived.

- *How easy did you find this exercise? On what basis did you identify the autobiographies?*
- *Are there particular moments in any of the extracts which seem more convincing or authentic to you, and why? Is it useful or even possible to establish authenticity?*
- *Turn to page 53 for further information about the passages. What new light does this throw upon the extracts and your answers to the questions?*

AUTOBIOGRAPHERS

Who writes autobiography and why? Publishers favour celebrities from the glamorous worlds of film, crime and politics. The fascination of autobiography is the insight it is supposed to give into those whose lives seem more thrilling than our own. What do they have that we have not? No matter how miserable or traumatised their lives have been, the coherent narrative makes the authors seem self-possessed and successful in spite of it all: 'authoritative' in every sense of the word. The autobiographer is engaging in a kind of fiction. The word 'I' conflates all the different aspects of self making the author seem more self-possessed than anyone actually feels. And the shaped narrative conceals the confusion of diverse experience. This fiction, of the self-possessed super-successful person, is attractive to a society which reveres the individual.

Many of the best-selling autobiographies are written by the rich and famous. Ordinary people have considered their own lives unworthy of the same attention and they have had neither the means nor the leisure to write. Publishers have in the past been so preoccupied with celebrities that the life stories of working class people have never been published for posterity. Their voices have, in effect, been silenced.

In recent years interest in the experiences of ordinary people has grown. James Brooke was encouraged by his daughter to write down his early memories of Dukinfield, his home town on the outskirts of Manchester. Now in his eighties he has published two pamphlets for the local community:

Of course, we had all the usual childhood ailments which our mothers treated with simple remedies. Toothache meant a baked potato, crushed and put in a sock, which you tied round your face with the potato to the affected part. If this was not successful, you paid a visit to the local chemist, Mr Avison, at the corner of King Street and Wharf Street, just facing the Queens. As far back as I can remember, Mr Avison was a very old man with a bald head, glasses on the end of his nose and a shuffling gait. You would go into his shop, ring the bell on the counter and it would seem an eternity before he appeared. You would then proceed to tell him what your trouble was, in this case that you had toothache and you wanted an extraction, and directing you to a straight-backed chair, he would potter off again into the house part. On his return he would ask you to point out the troublesome tooth, place his finger in your mouth and then you would realise that he was holding a pair of steel pliers in his hand because you heard them rattling on your teeth. He had a very shaky hand, but once he got a grip on the offending molar he would not let go. He twisted it forward, then a backward twist and pull with a jerk, and eureka! out would come the tooth. Finally, you were given a piece of tissue paper to wipe your mouth and another piece with your tooth in to take home. This was called 'extraction by cold steel' and cost 6d.

Those who could afford it might go to Mr Fish on Astley Street, just up from the Co-op stores. Now he was a proper dentist – qualified! However, he charged 9d for cold steel and 1s6d for a painless extraction. Of course, he was better equipped than Mr Avison, with a proper chair to sit in and a glass of pink warm water to wash your mouth out afterwards.

If you happened to be suffering from a troublesome cough you did not go to the doctor's, for that had to be paid for. Your mother sent you with a small bottle and 3d to George Hinchcliffe, the chemist at the corner of Mary Street next to the Newmarket Tavern, for threepennyworth of All Fours. Then you would take a cup to Mr Shaw's, the grocer's, for twopennyworth of black treacle. This was dissolved in a pint of boiling water, the All Fours mixture was added and the concoction poured into a pint bottle. After a few teaspoons of this, you soon got relief from your cough. To buy one pint bottle of All Fours cough mixture today would cost you pounds, yet the ingredients are just the same. [. . .]

In the late 1920s influenza epidemics were common. I have known whole mills to close down because of the absenteeism and sometimes hundreds died. Later, doctors advised inoculation and teams of nurses used to visit the places of employment for the purpose.

We once had a smallpox epidemic and what pandemonium that proved to be! Everybody with a pimple was reporting to their doctor and soon the isolation hospital in Hyde and the one near Hartshead Pike were full to overflowing. Every night outside the doctor's surgery there would be a queue of people waiting to be vaccinated, and afterwards you had to wear a red armband on that arm to warn people not to knock against you. The critical period of the vaccination was when it had formed a scab, for this had to drop off in its own time; if it was knocked off accidentally, you could have a very sore arm. It was so important to be vaccinated that this was the first thing the doctor asked you when you reported sick. If you had not been done, the doctor had not much patience with you. Complete mills were being disinfected against the complaint, and where there had been suspected smallpox in a home, the house was sealed up, fumigated with sulphur candles and kept sealed up for twenty-four hours.

(from *The Dukinfield I Knew* by James Brooke)

- *Do you consider there is any value in preserving the first-hand accounts of ordinary people leading ordinary lives? What use could or should be made of them?*
- *Why do you think there is a surge of interest in the autobiographies of ordinary people at the present time?*

THE PRIVATE SELF

To some extent, all work is autobiographical in the sense that writers draw upon their own experiences and views when they write. But most autobiography is a tailored presentation of self for the reading public. In presenting life stories – either as autobiography, biography or as documentary evidence – ethical problems can arise. This is particularly true when work is published without the approval of those concerned.

- *In a group, consider the arguments for and against publishing the following items:*
  a) *a biography which is unacceptable to the subject (for example, Anthony Holden's biography of Prince Charles);*
  b) *novels which are rumoured to be autobiographical (for example, the early intimate life of D. H. Lawrence is said to be represented in parts of* Sons and Lovers*);*
  c) *the posthumous publication of private papers such as personal letters and private diaries and notebooks (for example the diary of Franz Kafka or the letters of Keats to his lover);*
  d) *the posthumous publication of rejected manuscripts and early drafts (for example, poems by Philip Larkin which he rejected as too poor for publication or the manuscript of T. S. Eliot's* Wasteland *which includes long stretches of rejected and corrected material).*
- *Discuss the following two specific cases:*

The first is an extract from a diary kept by Samuel Pepys in 1663. Throughout this diary, he returns again and again to his jealous suspicions concerning his wife and her dancing master:

May 15.
... By coach to St. James's, and there told Mr Coventry what I had done with my Lord with great satisfaction, and so well pleased home, where I found it almost night, and my wife and the dancingmaster alone above, not dancing but talking. Now so deadly full of jealousy I am that my heart and head did so cast about and fret that I could not do any business possibly, but went out to my office, and anon late home again and ready to chide at every thing, and then suddenly to bed and could hardly sleep, yet durst not say any thing, but was forced to say that I had had news from the Duke concerning Tom Hater as an excuse to my wife, who by my folly has too much opportunity given her with that man, who is a pretty neat black man, but married. But it is a deadly folly and plague that I bring upon myself to be so jealous and by giving myself such an occasion more than my wife desired of giving her another month's dancing. Which however shall be ended as soon as I can possibly. But I am ashamed to think what a course I did take by lying to see whether my wife did wear drawers today as she used to do, and other things to raise my suspicion of her, but I found no true cause of doing it.

May 16.
Up with my mind disturbed and with my last night's doubts upon me, for which I deserve to be beaten if not really served as I am fearful of being, especially since God knows that I do not find honesty enough in my own mind but that upon a small temptation I could be false to her, and therefore ought not to expect more justice from her, but God pardon both my sin and my folly herein. To my office and there sitting all the morning, and at noon dined at home. After dinner comes Pembleton, and I being out of humour would not see him, pretending business, but, Lord! with what jealousy did I walk up and down my chamber listening to hear whether they danced or no.

(from *The Diaries of Samuel Pepys*)

- *What is your first reaction to this piece?*
- *This is a genuine diary entry. Samuel Pepys wrote it in cipher (a system of shorthand) and it was not decoded until 1825 by two scholars who then published the work. Does this influence the way you read the entry, and your feelings about doing so?*

The second example is a personal letter from the poet John Keats to Charles Brown, written on 1 November 1820 after arriving in Naples where he had reluctantly moved because of worsening tuberculosis, leaving behind his fiancée Fanny Brawne. He died four months later at the age of twenty-five.

Yesterday we were let out of Quarantine, during which my health suffered more from bad air and a stifled cabin than it had done the whole voyage. The fresh air revived me a little, and I hope I am well enough this morning to write to you a short calm letter; – if that can be called one, in which I am afraid to speak of what I would the fainest dwell upon. As I have gone thus far into it, I must go on a little; – perhaps it may relieve the load of

WRETCHEDNESS which presses upon me. The persuasion that I shall see her no more will kill me. I cannot q – My dear Brown, I should have had her when I was in health, and I should have remained well. I can bear to die – I cannot bear to leave her. Oh, God! God! God! Every thing I have in my trunks that reminds me of her goes through me like a spear. The silk lining she put in my travelling cap scalds my head. My imagination is horribly vivid about her – I see her – I hear her. There is nothing in the world of sufficient interest to divert me from her a moment. This was the case when I was in England; I cannot recollect, without shuddering, the time that I was prisoner at Hunt's, and used to keep my eyes fixed on Hampstead all day. Then there was a good hope of seeing her again – Now! – O that I could be buried near where she lives! I am afraid to write to her – to receive a letter from her – to see her hand writing would break my heart – even to hear of her any how, to see her name written would be more than I can bear. My dear Brown, what am I to do? Where can I look for consolation or ease? If I had any chance of recovery, this passion would kill me. Indeed through the whole of my illness, both at your house and at Kentish Town, this fever has never ceased wearing me out. When you write to me, which you will do immediately, write to Rome (poste restante) – if she is well and happy, put a mark thus +, — if—— Remember me to all. I will endeavour to bear my miseries patiently. A person in my state of health should not have such miseries to bear. Write a short note to my sister, saying you have heard from me. Severn is very well. If I were in better health I should urge your coming to Rome. I fear there is no one can give me any comfort. Is there any news of George? O, that something fortunate had ever happened to me or my brothers! – then I might hope, – but despair is forced upon me as a habit. My dear Brown, for my sake, be her advocate for ever. I cannot say a word about Naples; I do not feel at all concerned in the thousand novelties around me. I am afraid to write to her. I should like her to know that I do not forget her. Oh, Brown, I have coals of fire in my breast. It surprised me that the human heart is capable of containing and bearing so much misery. Was I born for this end? God bless her, and her mother, and my sister, and George, and his wife, and you, and all!

(from *Selected Letters and Poems of John Keats*)

- *What is your first reaction to this piece?*
- *Do you feel you have a right to read it?*
- *Whose responsibility is it to determine whether work of this nature should be published?*

Reading List

You will find the autobiographies of celebrities in any bookshop. We enjoyed *A Postillion Struck By Lightning* by film star Dirk Bogarde (Chatto and Windus, 1977). Simone de Beauvoir's trilogy (starting with *Memoirs of a Dutiful Daughter*) (Penguin, 1986) is generally considered a stimulating and important autobiography.
Examples of working class autobiographies are:
Truth, Dare or Promise edited by Liz Heron (Virago, 1985), which contains autobiographical writings by girls growing up in the fifties;

QueenSpark Books which are produced by people living in the Brighton area. Their aim is 'to publish autobiographies and other writing by people who would not normally find themselves in print.' There are similar publishing projects around the country and you could enquire at your library about projects in your area. The address of *QueenSpark Books* is Prior House, Tilbury Place, Brighton, Sussex.

The Dukinfield I Knew by James Brooke (1987) we have already mentioned. The extract used earlier in this chapter, in the section 'Autobiography as Fiction', comes from this locally published book. It is available at a reasonable cost from the publisher Neil Richardson, 375 Chorley Road, Swinton, Manchester.

There are several entertaining autobiographical books about childhood, recalling the past in wry anecdotes. We enjoyed:

Unreliable Memoirs, Clive James (Jonathan Cape, 1980)
Ash on A Young Man's Sleeve, Dannie Abse (Vallentine, Mitchell & Co., 1971)
Cider With Rosie, Laurie Lee (Hogarth Press, 1959)
There is A Happy Land, Keith Waterhouse (Michael Joseph, 1978)
I Know Why The Caged Bird Sings, Maya Angelou (Virago, 1984)

Two autobiographies which cast an interesting question mark over the nature of autobiography itself are:

Private Papers, Margaret Forster (Chatto and Windus, 1986)
Taking It Like A Woman, Ann Oakley (Fontana, 1985)

Letters and diaries are commonly available; indeed many politicians keep them expressly for later publication. Famous writers like John Keats, Virginia Woolf and Franz Kafka have had their private papers published: letters, diaries, manuscripts, notebooks and so on. Older diaries illuminate the attitudes of the past and suggest the texture of everyday life, for example, *The Diary of A Farmer's Wife (1796–7)* by Anne Hughes (Penguin, 1981). *Dear Girl* edited by Tierl Thompson (The Women's Press, 1987) contains the letters and diaries of two working class girls.

Notes on Extracts in 'Autobiography as Fiction'

1   *Free Fall* by William Golding (Faber and Faber, 1959) is a novel in which the central character writes a private account of his life.

2   *A Postillion Struck By Lightning* is the best-selling autobiography of Dirk Bogarde the actor (Triad Grafton, 1978).

3   *Taking It Like A Woman* is the autobiography of Annie Oakley, a feminist, sociologist and writer (Jonathan Cape, 1984).

4   This extract is also from the above autobiography. Different sections of the autobiography are related in different ways. This extract comes from occasional extracts which relate the events of a passionate but painful love affair.

5   *Private Papers* by Margaret Forster (Chatto and Windus, 1986) is a novel in which a daughter discovers her mother's private autobiographical writings and recounts her enraged reactions as she reads them.

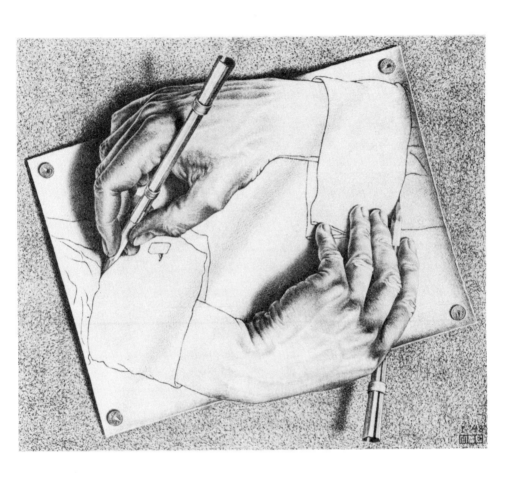

THE LIMITS OF LITERATURE

*L*ITERATURE AND MEANING

WORDS AND MEANINGS

It would be easy to think of language as a simple naming operation – a dictionary of words each of which represents something in reality. But language is much more complicated than this. Each word receives its meaning from its context. This is true of even the simplest of words. Consider the meaning of the word 'lost' in the following contexts:

– lost belongings;
– lost illusions;
– lost the road;
– lost the war;
– lost her father;
– feeling lost and lonely.

We also know a range of words conveying a similar meaning, and choose amongst them. There are subtle distinctions between 'grief' and 'sadness', 'misery' and 'mourning'. We know where misery ends because we have a sense of what sadness is and in what way it is different. We therefore define things not only by what they are, but more importantly by what they are *not*.

We tend to believe that language is fixed in relation to reality. The link between words and their meanings seems deceptively obvious. If we don't know how to say something or what a word means we only have to look it up in the guidebook to the system – the dictionary. Ironically, if you have a very good guidebook, like the thirteen volumes of the Oxford English Dictionary, it will actually show you that words have many possible meanings and that these meanings have changed over the years. For example, the word 'pride' – once the deadliest of the sins, (**pride** *comes before a fall*) is now a quality to be admired (*take* **pride** *in* *yourself*). This change mirrors wider changes in social attitudes. Individual qualities are valued much more in the modern trading economy than they were in the fixed hierarchies of feudal society. Unseemly ambition has now become praiseworthy individual endeavour. Even the most up-to-date guidebook cannot solve all problems of meaning. For example, what if no word exists for what we intend or what if the society we live in doesn't allow words to describe what we mean? What difficulties might one have in taking an open-minded attitude towards a 'gossip', 'bastard' or 'Communist', or to feel critical of the notion of 'mothering' or 'charity'? The words themselves are charged with associations picked up in social use. When we speak a language, we also speak the attitudes and assumptions with which it is loaded.

Meanings also arise from the context in which the words are used. If I say 'The cat is in the room', my meaning seems straightforward. But what does it mean if I scream it, or live in a culture which worships cats? What does it mean if I have just put the cat outside, or if there never was a cat at all? If meaning is so unstable, how can we ever trust that words mean what we think they mean? We only feel sure of meaning when we understand the social and cultural situation in which the words are expressed, and the relationship between speaker, language and listener.

The words themselves are quite arbitrary. As long as we all agree to use the word 'car' to describe the familiar motor vehicle, for example, we all know roughly what we mean. We could just as easily decide to call it a 'plumplush', but as long as we all used the same word, it wouldn't matter. Words are arbitrary symbols and they get their meanings from social use. Language is a social activity, not a collection of words. It reflects, expresses and defines the society which uses it.

- *Prepare a group presentation of the opening of Tom Stoppard's play* Cahout's Macbeth*:*

  Translation from 'Dogg' language into English is given in square brackets where this seems necessary.

Empty stage.
BAKER: (*Off-stage*) Brick! [*Here!]
    (*A football is thrown from off-stage left to off-stage right.*
    BAKER *receiving ball*) Cube. [*Thanks]
    (ABEL, *off-stage, throws satchel to stage left.* ABEL *enters. He is a schoolboy wearing grey flannel shorts, blazer, school cap, etc., and carrying a satchel. He drops satchel centre stage and collects the other which he places with his own.* ABEL *exits stage right and returns with microphone and stand which he places down stage. The microphone has a switch.*)
ABEL: (*Into the microphone*) Breakfast, breakfast . . . sun – dock – trog . . .
    [*Testing, testing . . . one – two – three . . .]

(He realizes the microphone is dead. He tries the switch a couple of times and then speaks again into the microphone.)
Sun – dock – trog – pan – slack . . . [*One – two – three – four – five . . .]
(The microphone is still dead. ABEL calls to someone off-stage.)
Haddock priest! [*The mike is dead!]
(Pause. BAKER enters from the same direction. He is also a schoolboy similarly dressed.)
BAKER: Eh? [*Eh?]
ABEL: Haddock priest.
BAKER: Haddock?
ABEL: Priest.
(BAKER goes to the microphone, drops satchel centre on his way.)
BAKER: Sun – dock – trog –
(The mike is dead. BAKER swears.) Bicycles!
(BAKER goes back off-stage. Pause. The loud-speakers crackle.)
ABEL: Slab? [*Okay?]
BAKER: *(Shouting off-stage, indistinctly.)* Slab!
ABEL: *(Speaking into the mike.)* Sun, dock, trog, slack, pan.
(The mike is live. ABEL shouting to BAKER, with a thumbs-up sign.)
Slab! [*Okay!]
(Behind ABEL, CHARLIE, another schoolboy, enters backwards, hopping about, the visible half of a ball-throwing game. CHARLIE is wearing a dress, but schoolboy's shorts, shoes and socks, and no wig.)
CHARLIE: Brick! . . . brick! [*Here! . . . here!]
(A ball is thrown to him from the wings. ABEL dispossesses CHARLIE of the ball.)
ABEL: Cube! [*Thanks!]
VOICE: *(Off-stage)* Brick! [*Here!]
(CHARLIE tries to get the ball but ABEL won't let him have it.)
CHARLIE: Squire! [*Bastard!]
(ABEL throws the ball to the unseen person in the wings – not where BAKER is.)
Daisy squire! [*Mean bastard!]
ABEL: Afternoons! [*Get stuffed!]
CHARLIE: *(Very aggrieved.)* Vanilla squire! [*Rotten bastard!]
ABEL: *(Giving a V-sign to CHARLIE.)* Afternoons!
(ABEL hopping about, calls for the ball from the wings.)
Brick! [*Here!]
(The ball is thrown to ABEL over CHARLIE's head. DOGG, the headmaster, in mortar-board and gown, enters from the opposite wing, and as the ball is thrown to ABEL, DOGG dispossesses ABEL.)
DOGG: Cube! [*Thank you!] Pax! [*Lout!]
(DOGG gives ABEL a clip over the ear and starts to march off carrying the ball.)
ABEL: *(Respectfully to DOGG.)* Cretinous, git? [*What time it is, sir?]
DOGG: *(Turning round.)* Eh?
ABEL: Cretinous pig-faced, git? [*Have you got the time please, sir?]
(DOGG takes a watch out of his waistcoat pocket and examines it.)
DOGG: Trog poxy. [*Half-past three.]
ABEL: Cube, git. [*Thank you, sir.]
DOGG: Upside artichoke almost Leamington Spa? [*Have you seen the lorry from Leamington Spa?]

ABEL: Artichoke, git? [*Lorry, sir?]
CHARLIE: Leamington Spa, git? [*Leamington Spa, sir?]
DOGG: Upside? [*Have you seen it?]
ABEL: (*Shaking his head.*) Nit, git. [*No, sir.]
CHARLIE: (*Shaking his head.*) Nit, git. [*No, sir.]
DOGG: (*Leaving again.*) Tsk. Tsk. [*Tsk. Tsk.] Useless. [*Good day.]
ABEL/CHARLIE: Useless, git. [*Good day, sir.]
    (DOGG *exits with the ball.* BAKER *enters. He looks at his wrist watch.*)
BAKER: Trog poxy. [*Half-past three.]
    (*There are now three satchels on the ground centre stage.* BAKER *goes to one and extracts a packet of sandwiches.* ABEL *and* CHARLIE *do the same. The three boys settle down and start to examine their sandwiches.*)
ABEL: (*Looking in his sandwiches.*) Pelican crash. [*Cream cheese.]
    (*To* BAKER.) Even ran? [*What have you got?]
BAKER: (*Looking in his sandwich.*) Hollyhocks. [*Ham.]
ABEL: (*To* CHARLIE.) Even ran? [*What have you got?]
CHARLIE: (*Looking in his sandwich.*) Mouseholes. [*Egg.]
ABEL: (*To* CHARLIE.) Undertake sun pelican crash frankly sun mousehole?
    [*Swop you one cream cheese for one egg?]
CHARLIE: (*With an amiable shrug.*) Slab. [*Okay.]
    (ABEL *and* CHARLIE *exchange half a sandwich each.*)
BAKER: (*To* ABEL.) Undertake sun hollyhocks frankly sun pelican crash?
ABEL: Hollyhocks? Nit!
BAKER: Squire!
ABEL: Afternoons!
    (BAKER *fans himself with his cap and makes a comment about the heat.*)
BAKER: Afternoons! Phew – cycle racks hardly butter fag ends.
    [*Comment about heat.]
CHARLIE: (*Agreeing with him.*) Fag ends likely butter consequential.
ABEL: Very true. [*Needs salt.]
CHARLIE: Eh?
ABEL: (*Putting out his hand.*) Very true.
    (CHARLIE *takes a salt cellar out of his satchel.* CHARLIE *passes* ABEL *the salt.*)
    Cube. [*Thank you.]
    (*He sprinkles salt on his sandwich and then offers salt to* BAKER.) Very true?
    [*Need salt?]
BAKER: (*Taking it.*) Cube. [*Thank you.]
    BAKER *uses the salt and puts it down next to him.* CHARLIE *puts his hand out towards* BAKER.)
CHARLIE: Brick. [*Here.]
    (BAKER *passes* CHARLIE *his salt-cellar. They eat their sandwiches.*)

- *Perform the extract for a group of people unfamiliar with the play and ask them to summarise the conversation. How easy do they find this?*
- *Use examples from the playscript to illustrate the ways meanings are made, beyond a simple knowledge of vocabulary.*

THE REFERENCES OF THE TEXT

'Twas this flesh begot those pelican daughters.

What do we understand by this comment made by King Lear in his hysterical reflection on his cruel children? Perhaps his daughters had long, thin legs? The cultural reference that makes sense of the comment is the image of the pelican children sucking blood from the parent. It is an image we might have encountered in literature or mythology, or a visual image we might have seen in a stained glass window. But is it common knowledge? For the reader, the problem lies in understanding the references made by the text, the knowledge it assumes we have. Editions of Shakespeare can feature as many explanatory notes as they do text.

- *Imagine you have been given a very thorough knowledge of the English language, but have not read any English Literature. You find the following piece of writing. You have little difficulty with the* literal *meaning of the words, but what questions do you need to ask in order to make sense of the writing?*

LEDA AND THE SWAN

A sudden blow: the great wings beating still
Above the staggering girl, her thighs caressed
By the dark webs, her nape caught in his bill,
He holds her helpless breast upon his breast.

How can those terrified vague fingers push
The feathered glory from her loosening thighs?
And how can body, laid in that white rush,
But feel the strange heart beating where it lies?

A shudder in the loins engenders there
The broken wall, the burning roof and tower
And Agamèmnon dead.
                        Being so caught up,
So mastered by the brute blood of the air,
Did she put on his knowledge with his power
Before the indifferent beak could let her drop?

W. B. Yeats

- *Do you feel you need further knowledge to arrive at an understanding of this poem? What factual information would help? What reading experiences do you need?*

There is a sense in which texts are always 'talking' about other texts: a sonnet makes sense to us as a sonnet because of its relationship to other poems, traditions and conventions, and because of the way in which it compares with other sonnets. A text may make its meaning through its reflections on a wide variety of other texts, such as myths, fairy tales and biblical stories. This accounts for one of the problems posed by models of 'good reading': often the text is not equally available to all, but is more available to an élite with more time and education for reading.

INTERPRETATIONS

Meanings do not reside solely within the poems, but also in the experience, knowledge and habits we bring to them. Readings are also influenced by the context in which we read. For example, consider your own reactions to the following poem:

AU JARDIN DES PLANTES

The gorilla lay on his back,
One hand cupped under his head,
Like a man.

Like a labouring man tired with work,
A strong man with his strength burnt away
In the toil of earning a living.

Only of course he was not tired out with work,
Merely with boredom; his terrible strength
All burnt away by prodigal idleness.

A thousand days, and then a thousand days,
Idleness licked away his beautiful strength
He having no need to earn a living.

It was all laid on, free of charge.
We maintained him, not for doing anything,
But for being what he was.

And so that Sunday morning he lay on his back,
Like a man, like a worn-out man,
One hand cupped under his terrible hard head.

Like a man, like a man,
One of those we maintain, not for doing anything,
But for being what they are.

A thousand days, and then a thousand days,
With everything laid on, free of charge,
They cup their heads in prodigal idleness.

John Wain

- *What effect might it have on your interpretation of the poem if*
  a) *you were unemployed?*
  b) *the poem had been written by one of your parents?*
  c) *you belonged to the Animal Liberation Front?*
  d) *you were a zoo keeper?*
  e) *you felt cooped up and bored yourself?*

Readers play a large part in reconstructing the meaning of the literature by bringing to it their own experiences, expectations and ideas. It is therefore a mistake to think that the meaning of literature lies completely within the text itself. If that were the case, the study of literature would be little more than the science of excavating the one true meaning. In fact, reading is more creative and personal than that. There are as many meanings as there are readers.

BEARINGS ON THE TEXT

We often start reading books with expectations based on previous information such as reviews we have read, other books by the same author or a film adaptation we have already seen. All this information primes our expectations and influences the way we read a book. It would be difficult to read Salman Rushdie's *Satanic Verses* without being alert to the accusations of blasphemy which earned him a death threat. Conversely, we are sometimes forced to re-evaluate a book in the light of new information. For example, when one discovers that George Eliot was a woman, one might well re-read *Middlemarch* with different expectations. By far the most common experience, however, is coming back to a text after some years only to discover that reactions on re-reading are quite different from the first occasion. The book has not changed; it is the reader who has changed. It is likely that a further reading after several years would be different again.

- *Read the following poems and discuss your reactions before turning to the end of this chapter for supplementary information.*

I
        Even such is time, which takes in trust
        Our youth, our joys, and all we have,
        And pays us but with age and dust:
        Who in the dark and silent grave
        When we have wandered all our ways
        Shuts up the story of our days.
        And from which earth and grave and dust
        The Lord shall raise me up, I trust.

2
Mine eyes have seen the glory of the coming of the Lord;
He is trampling out the vintage where the grapes of wrath are stored;
He hath loosed the fateful lightning of His terrible, swift sword;
    His truth is marching on.

I have seen Him in the watch-fires of a hundred circling camps;
They have builded Him an altar in the evening dews and damps;
I can read His righteous sentence by the dim and flaring lamps;
    His day is marching on.

I have read a fiery gospel, writ in burnished rows of steel:
'As ye deal with my contemners, so with you my grace shall deal;
Let the Hero, born of woman, crush the serpent with his heel,
  Since God is marching on.'

He has sounded forth the trumpet that shall never call retreat;
He is sifting out the hearts of men before His judgement-seat:
Oh, be swift, my soul, to answer Him! be jubilant, my feet!
  Our God is marching on.

In the beauty of the lilies Christ was born across the sea,
With a glory in His bosom that transfigures you and me:
As He died to make men holy, let us die to make men free,
  While God is marching on.

3   HEAVEN-HAVEN

I have desired to go
  Where springs not fail,
To fields where flies no sharp and sided hail
And a few lilies blow.

And I have asked to be
  Where no storms come,
Where the green swell is in the havens dumb,
And out of the swing of the sea.

● *Now read the information about these poems at the end of this section. Then
re-read the poems. In what way does the information change your reading
and interpretation?*

LITERATURE AS DOCUMENTARY

If meanings are largely determined by the reader, how reliable is
literature in illuminating the author, generation and society which
produced it? Some periods of history are well-documented. Others are
not. In the time of Julius Caesar, the world's largest library in
Alexandria was burned to the ground, destroying forever most of the
400,000 ancient texts which we will now never see.

Even the texts that survive are cryptic if we treat them as historical
witnesses, for we can never completely reconstruct the context in which
they were written and received. We can always make informed guesses,
but treating literature as documentary evidence has its dangers.

Imagine that a holocaust destroys present-day civilisation, and a
future generation very different from our own, and with very little
information about present-day society, excavates the fragments of
written material on pages 66 and 67. Tests confirm that the paper was
produced in the late twentieth century, and scholars are keen to
speculate about the nature of the society that produced them.

- *Put yourself in the position of a scholar in this future society and write an article for a scholarly magazine which analyses the fragments and attempts to generalise about the scholars, the literature and the society which produced them.*
- *Review the different interpretations placed upon the material by class members.*
- *How fair do you think some of the conclusions are?*
- *What problems does this activity suggest there are in using texts to draw conclusions about writers and the society in which they work?*
- *If you were called upon to select ten pieces of written material for a 'time capsule' to preserve for future generations a representative sample of literature today, what would you include? Discuss the principles upon which you would base your choice. Compare your selection with those of other class members and discuss what impression a future generation might gain from them.*

Reading List

Keywords by Raymond Williams (Flamingo, 1983) is an unusual dictionary of certain key words in our culture and explanations of how they have developed over the years.

Supplementary Information To Poems in 'Bearings on the Text'
1 This poem by Sir Walter Raleigh was found in his bible at the Gatehouse at Westminster the night before his execution.
2 This favourite hymn started life as the marching song of the Federal Party in the American War of Independence. It was composed by a woman, Julia Ward Howe, in 1862 and was known as the Battle Hymn of the Republic. Julia Ward Howe was a suffragette, a campaigner for world peace and a journalist who was considered to be outrageous and immoral.
3 This poem by Gerard Manley Hopkins is subtitled 'A Nun Takes the Veil'.

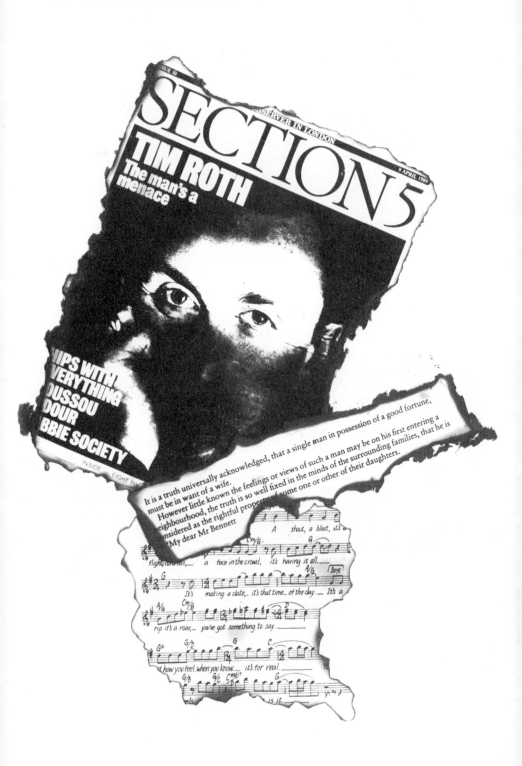

ACROSS:
1 Man with list puts the main point right in the back (9)
6 Hold-up arrest (4)
10 In rock hollow river cut shapes (5)
11 I act these out with a sense of beauty (9)
12 Chief adds liquid over victim's hot spot? (7)
13 Revolutionary transport from Mr. Carter (7)
14 Outcome of having a breather? (6,7)
17 Goat indicates guilty person who cannot get a hold? (6-7)
21 Noise in a large dwelling (7)
22 Porter, say, holding job as holy messenger (7)
24 Suffering in slump I can invest nothing for forceful advance (9)
25 Japanese ritual sport has to finish in decisive result (5)
26 Twist learner's put into stitch (4)
27 Where film directors produce a prickly environment? (9)

7 Favoured eventer running to come in the middle (9)
8 Animal with antlers and o with claws can be turned i harness (6)
9 As top sportsman I'm no ch rough up and jostle (8,6)
15 A bun in the oven? (6-3)
16 A banned drug to giv heavenly body? (8)
18 Stoical people break lence! (7)
19 Girl taken in fell bad soap (7)
20 Decay that is observ cles (6)
23 Dance beat, the curren

DOWN:
1 Campers carry it and crouch down beside fire (8)
2 Glutton's first to be covered in ood in big feed (5)
untry events which are com ed by whistle-stop tour? (8,6)
cised faulty set, in a way (7)
n who's entitled to serve up nan

Died some, pro patria,
non 'dulce' non 'et decor' . . .
walked eye-deep in hell
believing old men's lies, then unbelieving
came home, home to a lie,
ne to many deceits,
e to old lies and new infamy;
ge-old and age-thick
ers in public places

g as never before, wastage as never before.
ng blood and high blood,
heeks, and fine bodies;
ortitude as never before

frankness as never before,
disillusions as never told in the old days,
hysterias, trench confessions,
laughter out of dead bellies.

V

There died a myriad,
And of the best, among them
For an old bitch gone in the teeth,
For a botched civilisation.
Charm, smiling at the good mouth,
Quick eyes gone under earth's lid,

For two gross of broken statues,
For a f ousand battered books.

rustrated
ponse, A
ocket for
ghter. He
nd noticed
from the flame.
'I don't know how you and
your brothers created those
effects – the fire in the cellar,
e girl I thought was in the
ond. But then you're all very

clever, aren
He thrust the flame clo
her cheek. Christina recoiled,
turning her face aside, and the
car swerved dangerously. He
grabbed her wrist to steady the
wheel. There was something
peculiar about the flesh he
held. He looked down at her
hand and the unlit cigarette fell
from his lips, for the fing

ed loosely around the
ering wheel were no more
than blackened bone.
Christina's head slowly
turned towards him. Moonlight
clearly illuminated the other
side of her face. Ash screamed.
For her skin was charred and
withered, the fleshy lids
should have

THE ACT OF WRITING

THE WRITING PROCESS

Looking over the glossy covers and neat print of English literature, it is easy to forget that every set text emerged out of a process of composition which may have been difficult, messy and shifting in its intentions. Few writers start off with an inspired idea and write it up without encountering enormous challenges. Writing itself is a process which moulds and generates ideas.

For most people, the earliest experience of writing is in school. Because the examination system was dominated for many years by timed assignments, a premium was placed upon instant writing about topics chosen by an unknown examiner. Many teachers now feel students should be given more encouragement to write independently.

Review your own writing practices:

- *What are your earliest memories of writing?*
- *What preferences do you have about where, when and how you write?*
- *Compile all the writing you have done in the last week, including school work, shopping lists, diary entries and so on, and work out who initiates what proportion of your writing, for example, is it mainly other people? Work out also who are your readers: are they teachers, classmates, friends, yourself, or whom? Summarise your reasons for writing.*

Read the following piece which compares the arts of sculpture and writing, breaking your reading where indicated to discuss the questions in small groups:

Writing is a craft. Just as a painter works the canvas or a sculptor moulds the clay, the writer works with words. It is a three cornered process between writer, text and the reader within the writer. For most of writing is actually reading.

- *What do you notice when you watch someone writing? Do they write all the time? What else do they do? Notice in particular how the eyes move back over the work: what is the purpose of this re-reading?*

Imagine the sculptor fashioning a face of clay. The sculptor works, then stops, steps back, considers the effect. Noting something slightly wrong about the eyes, her fingers move back and adjust. In moments of frustration, she removes whole chunks of ear, eyelid and jawbone and begins again. In successful moments, she approves her own work and moves on to the details of the nose. The spectator inside her prompts the sculptor by casting a critical eye over the work as it proceeds.

- *Imagine this scenario with the writer as artist. What sort of adjustments does a writer make? What similarities do you see between the processes of sculpting and writing?*

All artists depend upon the quality of the critic within them, but they are also constrained by the time, experience and materials at their disposal. The sculptor works with clay, a medium which is tactile and visual, and works in three dimensions. It lends itself to certain projects. Every sculpture is created and judged in the light of other sculptures that have been made before. The writer however works with words.

- *What are the special features of writing as a medium? If sculpture is tactile and visual, what properties belong to the written word? What are its strengths and limitation?*

DRAFTING

The drafts on the next pages are the work of John Tomsett. The poem is a sonnet written in 1988 about the death of his wife's grandmother. Study the progress of the poem as it evolves through the drafts. We are indebted to the poet for this specially written commentary on the process of composition.

I.

She ironed each Sunday afternoon
The hot flat blade
Her ᵂᵒʳⁿ palm pushed the hot flat blade
A ritual. Collar, cuffs,
    That daughter is a mother too.
A ritual Kept religiously Simple

        religious ritual.

She died the day we wed
She'd iron each sunday at a afternoon
After lunch, her daughter by her ⋆side,
She'd Insist and moan with mock
                    mumble complaint.
Sometimes she
Insist and mumble mock complaint
    Her
That daughter acts as mother now
Prepares the board
        ensuring continuity.
Safegn· The hot flat blade moves
                    steadily.
    Ensuring Continuity.

DRAFT ONE

To begin the poem, I wrote down all the ideas and phrases that had been gathering in my mind about Annie and Pauline's ironing. On this first draft the movement of the sonnet is already established:

'She ironed each Sunday afternoon'
'Insist and moan with mock complaint'
'She died the day we wed'
'Her daughter acts as mother now'
'Ensuring continuity'

I decided to write the sonnet in iambic tetrameter (four beats to a line). Most sonnets are written in iambic pentameter (five beats to a line), but I like the shorter line – it sharpens the poetry, makes one use words more sparingly and search harder for the right word. At this stage, I was not concerned with rhyme. The final couplet, however, came almost complete, first go. Philip Larkin experienced, at times, a similar phenomenon when he wrote poetry:

I used to find that I was never sure I was going to finish a poem until I had thought of the last line. Of course, the last line was sometimes the first one you thought of!

Philip Larkin[1]

Unlike Larkin, I had the skeleton of the *whole* sonnet in front of me and it was a case of giving body and life to that frame.

2.

She'd iron each Sunday afternoon,
     After lunch   her daughter's guest
This
A willing skivvy would grin but
Insist and mumble mock complaint.
          perform
And always get her creases straight
         A nthal

Kept religiously

This willing skivvy would insist,
And Then grin and mumble mock complaint
Claiming she'd be sure
And Then claim that she'd be surely missed,—
She always got

This willing skivvy would insist
This willing skivvy would insist,
And grin in mumbled mock complaint
To claim that she'd be surely missed —
          And claim
When claiming
She always kept her creases straight.

DRAFT TWO

On the next draft, I worked on the second quatrain, concerning Annie's light-hearted complaints about her weight of work. There was no logic to the order in which I tackled parts of the poem. I was thinking about rhyme and rhythm and metre. It helps if you can get the iambic *beat* lodged in your mind – think *iambically* – then lines are formed more naturally in iambic metre (de-dum, de-dum, de-dum, de-dum). By the end of draft two the quatrain was virtually complete. I liked especially the phrase 'willing skivvy' – Annie would moan to me but *never* would she let someone else take over the ironing.

Her daughter's familys' clothes   3.

Shed stand, each Sunday, after lunch
Behind the her daughter's board

She ironed each Sunday afternoon
Her worn palm pushed the hot flat blade

A   ritual   kept religiously
A simple ritual, each Sunday

This willing skivvy would insist,
Then grin in mumbled mock complaint
And claim that shed be surely missed –
She always kept her creases straight.
She died the day we wed and now
Her daughter is our frequent guest

The hot flat blade moves steadily,
Ensuring continuity.

Each Sunday afternoon shed iron
for hous Her daughters' familys' clothes,

And now her daughter's
She died The day we wed and now
her daughter is our frequent guest

DRAFT THREE

Once I have a few lines almost complete I like to write them out at the beginning of the next draft, so that I can see the course the poem is taking. On the third draft I began to work out the first quatrain, whilst having the *completed* parts of the sonnet laid out on the page too. I'd connected the idea of Sunday and religious ceremony, with the wedding, the funeral and the ironing; as though Annie's ironing was as much a part of Sunday's rituals as her going to mass. I also liked the simplicity of the line, 'Her worn palm pushed the hot flat blade', which came from the first draft. I could not work out the whole of the quatrain, however. I kept thinking about Annie ironing 'after lunch'. It was only when I started to search for a rhyme for 'religiously' that I came up with 'tea', which solved the sticking point.

4.

Her worn palm pushed the hot flat blade,
A ritual kept religiously
Each Sunday afternoon For hours she stayed
Behind her daughters board til tea

Each Sunday afternoon she stayed
Behind her daughters board 'til tea
Her worn palm pushed the hot flat blade-
A ritual kept religiously.
This willing skivvy would insist,
Then grin in mumbled mock complaint
And claim that she'd be surely missed -
Who else could keep their creases straight?
She died the day we wed and now
Her daughter is our week-end guest,

The hot flat blade moves steadily,
Ensuring continuity.

Obedient she takes the board
And despite our pleas she shows whos best.
There is no doubt whose techniques best.
                    pleas
Despite our protests she won't allow
    Who, despite our pleas will she wont allow
    Despite our pleas she can't allow
And after lunch she shows us how
                    show us how

DRAFT FOUR

The four lines of the first quatrain come together at the top of the fourth draft. However, the four lines are in a different order from the finished quatrain. This was caused by the incompleteness of the 'Each Sunday afternoon...' line. The search for a rhyme with 'blade' found 'stayed', which completed the line and reorganized the quatrain. The final quatrain proved the most problematic. I wanted, somehow, to answer the question posed in line eight, without being explicit – the solution is obviously Pauline, Annie's daughter. *Tacit* continuity. I became hooked, however, on the 'how'/'allow' rhyme. I could not work things out. At this point I took a rest and came back to the sonnet a few hours later.

5.

She died the day we wed and now
Her daughter is our week-end guest,

The hot flat blade moves steadily
Ensuring continuity.

                          ~~she~~ vows
She is not bored

Who, despite our pleas will not allow

Who quietly, after lunch

She died the day that we were wed
And now her daughter lifts her hand
After lunch
She died soon after we were wed
And now ~~is~~ her daughter is our guest
For Sunday lunch; ~~with nothing said~~ no sooner
~~&~~ The board goes up without request.   fed,

DRAFT FIVE

Again the *completed* lines were set out. All the explorations from the bottom
of the previous draft were aborted and I began anew. The *solution* to the
quatrain came very quickly – returning to 'guest' and deciding to end the
first line with 'wed' helped enormously. 'Request' came as I wrote the line.
With the quatrain complete I rushed to set down the whole sonnet.

6.

Each sunday afternoon she stayed
Behind her daughter's board 'til tea –
Her worn palm pushed the hot flat blade:
A ritual kept religiously.
This willing skivvy would insist,
Then grin in mumbled mock complaint
And claim that she'd be surely missed –
Who else could keep their creases straight?
She died soon after we were wed
And now her daughter is our guest
For sunday lunch; no sooner fed,
The board goes up without request.
The hot flat blade moves steadily,
~~Ensuring~~ continuity.
In tacit

DRAFT SIX

When I had written out the sonnet in its entirety, I decided to make the change in the final line. 'Ensuring' was too obvious, too self-conscious, too explicit. Pauline's ironing was a far more subtle act, performed quietly, with reverence, I think 'tacit' reflects this important point.

7.

Natural Instinct   Sunday Rithal   Filial
        Rithal   Sundays.
                                    Sunday Service

Continuity

```
Each sunday afternoon she stayed
Behind her daughter's board 'til tea:       Traditions.
Her worn palm pushed the hot flat blade;
A ritual kept religiously.
This willing skivvy would insist,
Then grin in mumbled mock complaint
And claim that she'd be surely missed -
Who else could keep their creases straight?
She died soon after we were wed
And now her daughter is our guest
For sunday lunch; no sooner fed
The board goes up, without request.
The hot flat blade moves steadily,
In tacit continuity.
```

Mother's Day

(Mothering Sundays)

in memorium A.N., 1906-1988

DRAFT SEVEN

When a poem is virtually complete I like to see it in type, so that there is nothing between me and the words on the page. I originally intended this sonnet to partner another piece under the title 'Rituals'. The other sonnet concerned us experiencing both a wedding and a funeral in the same week. However, I was not happy with the other sonnet and decided 'Mothering Sundays' should stand on its own. The title was the result of an hour's deep contemplation.

AFTERWORD

Sometimes, when a sonnet is not going to work, it is because there is no *life* in the words; the rhyme dictates the path of the poem and the course of the poem lacks *true* definition. The poem is devoid of real *energy* and only finds its definition as a sonnet by the rigours of the rhyme and the exact number of lines, by the *shape* of the piece on the page. In a recent radio interview Seamus Heaney highlighted this major problem of writing within the sonnet *form* without finding the *live* element:

> There is a mistaken equivalence being made nowadays in this kind of talk about return to form. A lot of people mean they are using shapes. I think that a sonnet, for example, isn't fourteen lines that rhyme. A sonnet is a system of muscles and enjambments and eight and six – it's got a waist in the middle. It is a form. [In a shaped sonnet] there are indeed fourteen lines and there are indeed rhymed words at the end, but the actual move or the movement of the stanza, the movement of the sonnet, isn't there. So I would make a distinction between form, which is an act of living

principle, and shape *which is discernible on the page but inaudible and kinetically, muscularly unavailable. Poetry is a muscular response, I feel. You read a Shakespeare sonnet, a beloved Shakespeare sonnet, it's a dance within yourself.*

Seamus Heaney[2]

I feel that *'Mothering Sundays'* works because it is a *living* entity, the movement of the sonnet is there. Of the poems I have written, it is one of my most cherished.

John Tomsett

NOTES

1 An Interview with *Paris Review*, REQUIRED WRITING, p. 58 (Faber & Faber, 1983).
2 *'A Common Language'* – An Interview with Seamus Heaney, Derek Walcott, Les Murray, and Joseph Brodsky. KALEIDOSCOPE (BBC Radio 4, April, 1988).

● *Reread the drafts in the light of John Tomsett's commentary and consider the following points:*
   a) where the ideas originated and how they began to germinate;
   b) how the meaning developed and changed in the course of drafting;
   c) how far the developing poem was constrained and/or assisted by the sonnet form.

A SENSE OF PURPOSE

Writing is rarely spontaneous and never free of constraints. It is tailored to the expected reader, the purpose of the piece and the context in which it will be read or published.

● *Can you think of other factors which influence the way people write?*

● *Here are a number of extracts to read and discuss. For whom do you think they are written? When and where do you expect they will be read and for what purpose? What do you suppose is the writer's purpose in each case?*

1 John Chambers asked LB what had happened over the last 6 months. Mr Cadman reported that consultation had been carried out with ICC and various possibilities had been discussed, including the routing of the Holly Estate Hoppa service via St James's Road. None of the alternatives had proved practicable. It was agreed that LRT would request LBH to allow re-routing of 37 via Green Corner.

2 And a woman who held a babe against her bosom said, Speak to us of Children.

And he said:
Your children are not your children.
They are the sons and daughters of Life's longing for itself.
They come through you but not from you.
And though they are with you yet they belong not to you.
You may give them your love but not your thoughts,
For they have their own thoughts.
You may house their bodies but not their souls,
For their souls dwell in the house of tomorrow, which you cannot visit, not
even in your dreams.
You may strive to be like them, but seek not to make them like you.
For life goes not backward nor tarries with yesterday.
You are the bows from which your children as living arrows are sent forth.

3 Like analepses, prolepses can refer either to the same character, event, or
storyline figuring at that point in the text (homodiegetic) or to another
character, event or story-line (heterodiegetic). Again like analepses, they can
cover either a period beyond the end of the first narrative (external), or a
period anterior to it but posterior to the point at which it is narrated
(internal), or combine both (mixed).

4 4.00 'Daddy, you're a cake.' Alexander's wit is rather hard to take at this
hour in the morning. G and I keep eyes tight shut and pretend to be asleep.
   'And Mummy's a sandwich.
   'MUMMY! YOU'RE A SANDWICH!'
   'Mummy's a very tried sandwich Alexander.'
   'No you're not.'
   'Yes I am. And Daddy is a very tired cake. Look – the cake's asleep. The
cake and the sandwich are going to have some more sleep or they won't be
able to play games in the morning.' Pause.

   4.10 'I'm a tractor and I'm going to crash you. I'M GOING TO CRASH
YOU. AND I WANT MY CORNFLAKES.'
   Katie stirring and Rory starting to beat up for another feed so we decide to
abandon the rest of the night and take Alexander downstairs for a pre-dawn
breakfast.

As can be seen from this brief outline of a recent thankfully fairly unusual
night in our house there can be no guarantee of peaceful nights with children
of any age.

● *Discuss your answers and then consider the factors which led to your
conclusions. Say what aspects of the writing are tailored for their particular
audience and purpose, and illustrate your answers with details from the
extracts. Further details about these extracts can be found on page 79.*

Reading List

Writers themselves offer the best insight into the writing process. Visit the British Museum Manuscript Room where the draft manuscripts of many writers, composers and designers are on display: the drafts of Wordsworth, Dickens, Austen, Mozart and the notebooks of Leonardo da Vinci are of particular interest. Museums dedicated to particular writers often contain manuscripts, as do the larger regional museums.

The drafts of some important works are available in print. If you are studying *The Waste Land* by T. S. Eliot, for example, you might find it useful to look at the drafts with Pound's editing comments, published by Faber.

For the testimony of writers, try the following:

The second section of *The Cool Web* edited by Meek, Warlow and Barton (The Bodley Head, 1978) contains fascinating interviews with authors about their methods of composition. Enid Blyton and Phillipa Pearce turn in interesting evidence.

Vladimir Mayakovsky's *How Are Verses Made?* (Jonathan Cape, 1970) is short and practical. It passes on examples and ideas about the way poems germinate and develop.

Ted Hughes' *Poetry in the Making* (Faber and Faber, 1969) contains the background to many of his best known poems. It is a practical and accessible book.

Extracts used in 'A Sense of Purpose'
1 is from the minutes of a Local Residents Association meeting.
2 is from *The Prophet* by Kahlil Gibran, a book of inspirational poetry.
3 is from *Narrative Fiction* by Shlomith Rimmon-Jenan, an academic book about literature.
4 is from *Silent Night* by Jane Asher, a child care handbook for parents with sleepless children.

THE STRUCTURE OF TEXTS

THE LOGIC OF LANGUAGE

Everyday actions depend upon our conviction that they have consequences. We kick a football and it flies off through the air. One can't prove the connection, but our approach to science allows us to believe in it. Indeed this belief in cause and effect runs very deep in our culture. It is a different approach to the material world than that held by certain other cultures who believe that outcomes are determined by God or by Fate, and others who consider the link between cause and effect to be at best a tenuous or ambiguous one.

Cause and effect is embedded in our language and in our literature, firstly because the syntax of our language assumes it ('He kicked the ball sky high') and secondly because our dominant form of literature is narrative which is based on the cause-and-effect chain ('and then he did this . . . and so that happened . . . and she responded by . . . and he countered with . . .'

- *Here are two poems presented out of line order except for the first line. Try reassembling each of them into their original order and verses.*

I   NOTHING TO BE SAID – a poem in three stanzas

     A.   For nations vague as weed (*first line*)
     B.   Or birth, advance
     C.   Nothing to be said.
     D.   For nomads among stones,
     E.   The day spent hunting pig
     F.   Hours giving evidence
     G.   On death equally slowly.

H. So are their separate ways
I. Of building, benediction,
J. In mill-towns on dark mornings
K. Life is slow dying.
L. And cobble-close families.
M. Ways of slow dying.
N. And saying so to some
O. Measuring love and money
P. Or holding a garden-party.
Q. Small-statured cross-faced tribes
R. Means nothing; others it leaves

2   THE PULLEY – a poem in four stanzas

A. When God at first made man, (*first line*)
B. Contract into a span.
C. Rest in the bottome lay.
D. Bestow this jewell also on my creature,
E. If goodnesse lead him not, yet wearinesse
F. Having a glasse of blessings standing by;
G. But keep them with repining restlessnesse:
H. He would adore my gifts instead of me,
I. When almost all was out, God made a stay,
J. Perceiving that alone of all his treasure
K. May tosse him to my breast.
L. Then beautie flow'd, then wisdome, honour, pleasure:
M   So strengthe first made a way;
N. Let us (said he) poure on him all we can:
O. Yet let him keep the rest,
P. So both should losers be.
Q. Let him be rich and wearie, that at least,
R. Let the worlds riches, which dispersed lie,
S. For if I should (said he)
T. And rest in Nature, not the God of Nature:

You can check your final version against the originals at the end of the chapter.

- *Discuss the logical development of the original poems. You may find it useful to consider the following aspects:*
  a) *the relative difficulty of reassembling each poem;*
  b) *what kind of cues you looked for;*
  c) *what happened in the absence of cues during the exercise;*
  d) *the effect on the reader of an assembled poem which is deliberately devoid of cues.*

It is interesting to consider the way language both informs and expresses our habitual ways of thinking. There are obvious differences between language used in different historical periods, which express the attitudes of the time. Recent research suggests there may be differences between the language used by men and women, suggesting that men are inclined to express themselves in conventional 'cause-and-effect' language, whereas women are more inclined to connect things by metaphor, allusion and association.

A rich area of study in literature is the way novels develop. The cause-and-effect progress of the plot may be counterpointed by a different kind of logic running beneath – a logic of symbolism, contrasts and relationships. Feminist critics have placed particular importance upon these aspects in women's fiction. A novel as familiar as *Jane Eyre* for example has been illuminated and re-interpreted by criticism of this sort.

FORM AND MEANING

All texts have an underlying shape or logic of their own. Take the sonnet as an example. You probably already know that a sonnet has fourteen lines. It is an attractive format because its fourteen lines are compact and disciplined but also versatile for dividing up and shaping the argument. Some poets have used the first eight lines to develop an opening line of thought and the remaining six to throw it into a new perspective. This is sometimes known as the Petrarchan sonnet. Others have preferred to structure the sonnet in three quatrains (groups of four lines) and to round them off with a resounding couplet at the end. The feel of such sonnets – Shakespearean sonnets – is quite different from the Petrarchan ones.

- *Consider John Tomsett's sonnet on page 76. What is the structure of that sonnet and how apt is it for the thoughts developed in it?*

Here is another sonnet, written in the early part of the seventeenth century. The poet calls upon God to save him from the terrors of approaching death by forgiving him his sins and restoring his faith.

- *Look carefully at the structure of thought in this sonnet, and in particular at the choice and arrangement of rhymes:*

> Thou hast made me, and shall Thy work decay?
> Repair me now, for now mine end doth haste,
> I run to death, and death meets me as fast,
> And all my pleasures are like yesterday;
> I dare not move my dim eyes any way,
> Despair behind, and death before doth cast
> Such terror, and my feeble flesh doth waste
> By sin in it, which it towards hell doth weigh;
> Only Thou art above, and when towards Thee

By Thy leave I can look, I rise again;
But our old subtle foe so tempteth me
That not one hour myself I can sustain;
Thy Grace may wing me to prevent his art,
And Thou like adamant draw mine iron heart.

John Donne

- *In groups, discuss the choice and pattern of rhymes in the sonnet, and examine how far they support and express the poet's line of thought.*
- *Look further into the sonnet and note other aspects of the language, such as the vocabulary and the rhythm, which manifest the pattern of thought.*

Sonnets offer clear examples of the way meanings are generated by form. The relationship between language, form and meaning is one of mutual dependence. Meanings do not dress up in language: it is the language which constitutes the meaning.

- *Finally, read this poem by Philip Larkin and discuss how the pattern of thought is manifested in the language and form:*

WIRES

The widest prairies have electric fences,
For though old cattle know they must not stray
Young steers are always scenting purer water
Not here but anywhere. Beyond the wires

Leads them to blunder up against the wires
Whose muscle-shredding violence gives no quarter.
Young steers become old cattle from that day,
Electric limits to their widest senses.

MAPPING TEXTS

When we look at a complete text, complex patterns of meaning may emerge. Narrative, for example, may unfold in a cause-and-effect chain, whilst the mood and tempo may fluctuate and the characters shift in their relationships to one another. It can be interesting to map out some of these relationships in diagrams. Look at pages 84 and 85.

- *Try mapping out some aspects of texts you have studied recently. For example, try showing:*
  a) the relationships of characters to each other;
  b) the development of the plot;
  c) the relationship between characters, themes and events.

Such diagrams are effective as aide-memoires, but they can also

THE ENDING OF <u>EMMA</u> - a cliche and a cop-out

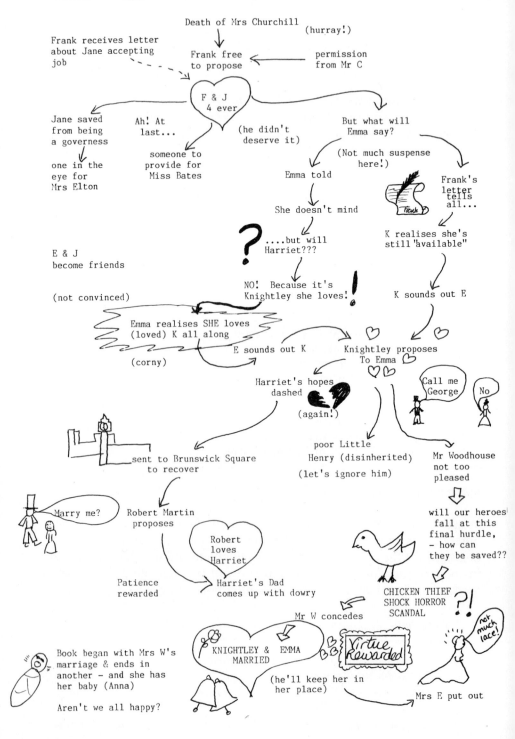

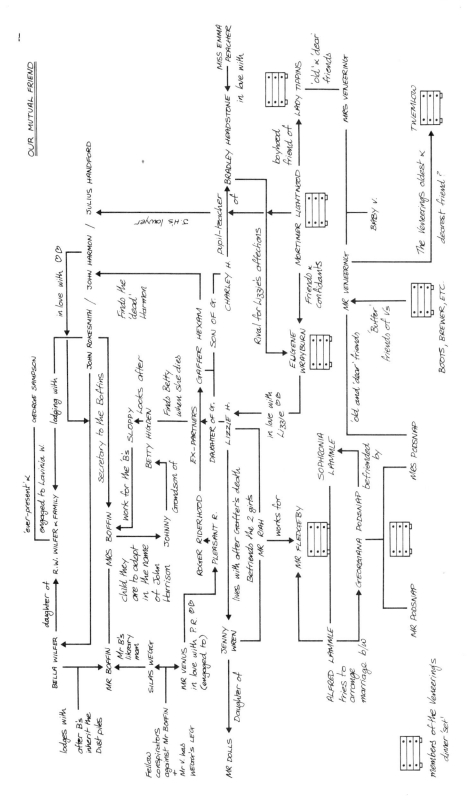

point to underlying features of a text, such as deliberate comparisons between characters and situations, or the sequence of high points in a serialised novel.

NARRATIVE STRUCTURE

Narrative can be seen as a simple progression, one event following another leading to a resolution. It could be argued that the underlying pattern of all narratives is to move from expectation to satisfaction: for example, a story of a mystery ending with a revelation. Even the briefest account can follow this route:

> The baby cried. The mommy picked it up.

Harold Rosen argues that this tiny narrative has all the features of a story and that these features can be applied to the analysis of more sophisticated texts. It has:
- events (here the two acts of the story);
- a storyline (the order in which the events are unfolded);
- an act of narration (the way the story is told).

Close study may reveal interesting discrepancies between the different elements of a narrative. For example, the *storyline* might be used to withhold events, focusing only on certain events and obscuring others. The time structure of the narrative can move backwards or forwards, 'cut' time, dwell extensively on an event or represent the actual passing of time. In studying the act of narration, we might notice how far the narrator is removed from the events, and how trustworthy is his or her account. In a text which aims to be realistic, we tend not to expect difficulties or discrepancies, and they are glossed over by both the writer and the reader.

It is always worth inspecting a text for its particular gaps, emphases, evasions and mysteries, for they may point to meanings other than those first offered. For example, a Sherlock Holmes story offers the traditional satisfactions of narrative, moving from mystery to explanation to resolution. But there are often aspects of the stories which are unexplored and unexplained, such as the motivation of criminals and the haunting sexuality of the female characters. These may reveal 'unconscious' meanings in the stories, such as the criminality of the working classes and a fear of women.

Another type of story which illustrates the fascination of narrative is the modern myth. This is a story which circulates by word of mouth which people always describe as 'true' but which is never authenticated. Such stories are sometimes called 'urban myths', and they seem to play on everyday anxieties. Consider this story which was told all over America and Europe in the 1950s. How well does it illustrate the features of narrative structure – storyline, events and the act of narration – outlined above?

> My sister-in-law has this friend, and she knows a couple who drive out of town most nights to do their courting in the back of his Dad's car. They go down a quiet lane which is often used by courting couples. Well, one evening they were up to their usual tricks when the music on the radio suddenly stopped, and there was a newsflash that a murderer had escaped from the local mental hospital. This murderer was highly dangerous, and listeners were warned to keep away from him. He had an unusual distinguishing feature: a hook instead of his right hand. The girlfriend got upset, especially as the hospital was quite close by, and wanted to drive off to somewhere safer, but her boyfriend said there was no need to worry: 'Let's just wind up the windows,' he said, 'and lock the doors, and nobody will be a bit interested in us'. But the girlfriend thought she could hear noises around the car, and got so upset she broke down into tears, so that in the end he had to drive her home. Once they'd arrived back at her parents' house, she calmed down and they had a last lingering goodnight kiss. Finally, she got out of the car and turned to shut the door when she screamed and fell down in a faint. There, hanging from the door handle was a large hook.

- *Go through the story and pick out or list the actual **events** of the story in the order they occur.*
- *Now consider the **story** as a whole.*
  What else is included in the text besides the actual events?
  The reader is invited to draw certain conclusions which are not actually stated. What are these?
  What attitudes are there in the story towards mental illness, courtship and the nature of men and women?
- *Now consider the **narration**.*
  Say this story is told to you by a friend claiming a second-hand acquaintance with the victims. What effect does this have on your attitude towards the story?
  From whose perspective is the story told?
  Are there elements of this story which are emphasised disproportionately to their role in the storyline? How do you explain this?
  Notice the way time is used in the story. Which events are described speedily, slowly, ignored?
  What is the implied 'truth' behind the story and what is left unresolved, unexplored or unexplained?
- *Spend a few minutes exchanging modern myths in circulation at the present time. Select the most fascinating story and repeat the above exercise. What do you think can be gained from such analysis?*

Reading List

For a short look at narrative analysis, try *Stories and Meanings* by Harold
Rosen (NATE).

Reassembled poems from 'The Logic of Language'

I   NOTHING TO BE SAID

> For nations vague as weed,
> For nomads among stones,
> Small-statured cross-faced tribes
> And cobble-close families
> In mill-towns on dark mornings
> Life is slow dying.
>
> So are their separate ways
> Of building, benediction,
> Measuring love and money
> Ways of slow dying.
> The day spent hunting pig
> Or holding a garden-party.
>
> Hours giving evidence
> Or birth, advance
> On death equally slowly.
> And saying so to some
> Means nothing; others it leaves
> Nothing to be said.

Philip Larkin

2   THE PULLEY

> When God at first made man,
> Having a glasse of blessings standing by;
> Let us (said he) poure on him all we can:
> Let the worlds riches, which dispersed lie,
>   Contract into a span.
>
> So strength first made a way;
> Then beautie flow'd, then wisdome, honour, pleasure:
> When almost all was out, God made a stay,
> Perceiving that alone of all his treasure
>   Rest in the bottome lay.
>
> For if I should (said he)
> Bestow this jewell also on my creature,
> He would adore my gifts instead of me,
> And rest in Nature, not the God of Nature:
>   So both should losers be.

Yet let him keep the rest,
But keep them with repining restlessnesse:
Let him be rich and wearie, that at least,
If goodnesse leade him not, yet wearinesse
May tosse him to my breast.

George Herbert

THE EDGE OF MEANING

REALISM

When a piece of literature is described as 'realistic', it is almost certainly intended as a word of praise. But what does it mean, to be 'realistic'? And why are we fascinated by things simply because they are 'realistic'?

'Realism' is a term which used to be used to describe the style of novels in the nineteenth century. At this time, novels were preoccupied with the material world and the way lives were shaped by external forces such as environment, society and family. It attempted to record the texture of life in that society, even where it was seamy and impoverished. Although its detail is persuasive, it is nonetheless selective. It is just one version of the world about us. Today the term 'realism' is used more loosely, though many novels and television programmes still try to represent the 'material' world by reproducing it in faithful detail, by using everyday styles of dialogue and by retaining a concern for social issues. It is the dominant style of fiction and is so familiar that it seems the natural and obvious way to write. This has posed great problems for writers who have new things to say which can't be conveyed in the realist mode. Not least of these problems is that they get labelled as 'experimental'. Realism is so dominant that every other literary style is regarded as a fringe activity and is often difficult to comprehend.

The main purpose of the following activity is to define what it is you mean when you speak of 'realism', and to identify those qualities you associate with it. Here are some extracts which all have some claim on the term 'realistic'. As you read them, compile a list of features considered to be 'realistic'.

This is the opening of *Sentimental Education* by Gustave Flaubert who is considered one of the foremost French realist writers, translated by Robert Baldick:

On the 15th of September 1840, at six o'clock in the morning, the *Ville-de-Montereau* was lying alongside the Quai Saint-Bernard, ready to sail, with clouds of smoke pouring from its funnel.

People came hurrying up, out of breath; barrels, ropes and baskets of washing lay about in everybody's way; the sailors ignored all inquiries; people bumped into one another; the pile of baggage between the two paddle-wheels grew higher and higher; and the din merged into the hissing of the steam, which, escaping through some iron plates, wrapped the whole scene in a whitish mist, while the bell in the bows went on clanging incessantly.

At last the boat moved off; and the two banks, lined with warehouses, yards, and factories, slipped past like two wide ribbons being unwound.

A long-haired man of eighteen, holding a sketchbook under his arm, stood motionless beside the tiller. He gazed through the mist at spires and buildings whose names he did not know, and took a last look at the Île Saint-Louis, the Cité, and Notre-Dame; and soon, as Paris was lost to view, he heaved a deep sigh.

The famous whaling yarn, *Moby Dick*, was written by Herman Melville who had himself sailed the South Seas in the whaling ship *Acushnet*:

In the first place, the enormous cutting tackles, among other ponderous things comprising a cluster of blocks generally painted green, and which no single man can possibly lift – this vast bunch of grapes was swayed up to the main-top and firmly lashed to the lower mast-head, the strongest point anywhere above a ship's deck. The end of the hawser-like rope winding through these intricacies, was then conducted to the windlass, and the huge lower block of the tackles was swung over the whale; to this block the great blubber hook, weighing some one hundred pounds, was attached. And now suspended in stages over the side, Starbuck and Stubb, the mates, armed with their long spades, began cutting a hole in the body for the insertion of the hook just above the nearest of the two side-fins. This done, a broad, semicircular line is cut round the hole, the hook is inserted, and the main body of the crew striking up a wild chorus, now commence heaving in one dense crowd at the windlass. When instantly, the entire ship careens over on her side; every bolt in her starts like the nailheads of an old house in frosty weather; she trembles, quivers, and nods her frightened mast-heads to the sky. More and more she leans over to the whale, while every gasping heave of the windlass is answered by a helping heave from the billows; till at last, a swift, startling snap is heard; with a great swash the ship rolls upwards and backwards from the whale, and the triumphant tackle rises into sight dragging after it the disengaged semicircular end of the first strip of blubber. Now as the blubber envelops the whale precisely as the rind does an orange, so is it stripped off from the body precisely as an orange is sometimes stripped by spiralizing it. For the strain constantly kept up by the windlass continually keeps the whale rolling over and over in the water, and as the blubber in one strip uniformly peels off along the line called the 'scarf,' simultaneously cut by the spades of Starbuck and Stubb, the mates; and just as fast as it is thus peeled off, and indeed by the very act itself, it is all the time being hoisted higher and higher aloft till its upper end grazes the main-top; the men at the windlass then cease heaving, and for a moment or two the prodigious blood-dripping mass sways to and fro as if let down from the sky, and every one present must take good heed to dodge it when it swings, else it may box his ears and pitch him headlong overboard.

Much of the literature currently being written in Asia and Latin America is known as magical realism, because it combines features from fairy-tale with contemporary political issues. In this case, Isabel Allende – the niece of Salvador Allende, the murdered elected president of Chile – founds her story on the crisis which brought democracy to an end in Chile and installed a military dictatorship there. The novel is entitled *The House of the Spirits*. This translation is by Magda Bogin:

She was absorbed in the task of tracking down the disappeared, comforting the victims of torture who returned with their backs flayed and their eyes unfocused, and searching for food for the priests' soup kitchens. Still, in the silence of the night, when the city lost its stage-set normality and operetta peace, she was besieged by the agonizing thoughts she had repressed during the day. At that time of night, the only traffic consisted of trucks filled with bodies and detainees, and police cars that roamed the streets like lost wolves howling in the darkness of the curfew. Alba shook in her bed. She saw the ghosts of all those unknown dead, heard the great house pant with the labored breath of an old woman. Her hearing sharpened and she felt the dreadful noises in her bones: a distant screeching of brakes, the slam of a door, gunfire, the crush of boots, a muffled scream. Then the long silence would return, lasting until dawn, when the city reawakened and the sun seemed to erase the terrors of the night. She was not the only one in the house who lay awake at night. She often came upon her grandfather in his nightshirt and slippers, older and sadder than during the day, heating up a cup of bouillon and muttering the curses of a buccaneer because his bones and his soul were killing him. Her mother also rummaged in the kitchen or walked like some midnight apparition through the empty rooms.

Thus the months went by, and it became clear to everyone, even Senator Trueba, that the military had seized power to keep it for themselves and not to hand the country over to the politicians of the right who had made the coup possible.

In *Down and Out in Paris and London* George Orwell writes about his experiences during the Depression of 1933. As an active political journalist, part of his purpose was to expose the appalling conditions of the poor and to stimulate social conscience to bring about change. Here he describes his experiences as a *plongeur* (or dishwasher) in a Paris hotel:

My bad day was when I washed up for the dining-room. I had not to wash the plates, which were done in the kitchen, but only the other crockery, silver, knives and glasses; yet, even so, it meant thirteen hours' work, and I used between thirty and forty dishcloths during the day. The antiquated methods used in France double the work of washing up. Plate-racks are unheard-of, and there are no soap-flakes, only the treacly soft soap, which refuses to lather in the hard, Paris water. I worked in a dirty, crowded little den, a pantry and scullery combined, which gave straight on the dining-room. Besides washing up, I had to fetch the waiters' food and serve them at table; most of them were intolerably insolent, and I had to use my fists more than once to get common civility. The person who normally washed up was a woman, and they made her life a misery.

It was amusing to look round the filthy little scullery and think that only a double door was between us and the dining-room. There sat the customers in all their splendour – spotless table-cloths, bowls of flowers, mirrors and gilt cornices and painted cherubim; and here, just a few feet away, we in our disgusting filth. For it really was disgusting filth. There was no time to sweep the floor till evening, and we slithered about in a compound of soapy water, lettuce-leaves, torn paper and trampled food. A dozen waiters with their coats off, showing their sweaty armpits, sat at the table mixing salads and sticking their thumbs into the cream pots. The room had a dirty, mixed smell of food and sweat. Everywhere in the cupboards, behind the piles of crockery, were squalid stores of food that the waiters had stolen. There were only two sinks, and no washing basin, and it was nothing unusual for a waiter to wash his face in the water in which clean crockery was rinsing. But the customers saw nothing of this. There were a coconut mat and a mirror outside the dining-room door, and the waiters used to preen themselves up and go in looking the picture of cleanliness.

It is an instructive sight to see a waiter going into a hotel dining-room. As he passes the door a sudden change comes over him. The set of his shoulders alters; all the dirt and hurry and irritation have dropped off in an instant. He glides over the carpet, with a solemn priest-like air. I remember our assistant *maître d'hôtel*, a fiery Italian, pausing at the dining-room door to address an apprentice who had broken a bottle of wine. Shaking his fist above his head he yelled (luckily the door was more or less soundproof):

'*Tu me fais* – Do you call yourself a waiter, you young bastard? You a waiter! You're not fit to scrub floors in the brothel your mother came from. *Maquereau!*'

Words failing him, he turned to the door; and as he opened it he farted loudly, a favourite Italian insult.

Then he entered the dining-room and sailed across it dish in hand, graceful as a swan.

- *In a group, compile a list of subjects and stylistic features you commonly associate with the term 'realistic'.*
- *What is the appeal of the 'realistic'?*
- *Give examples of work you consider to be 'unrealistic'. Is it unappealing to be 'unrealistic'?*
- *Re-present one of the passages from a different viewpoint like this:*
  a) the inner thoughts of Flaubert's young man as we watch him, for example as a stream-of-consciousness monologue;

b) *an account of the 'cutting in' by someone committed to the conservation of whales;*
c) *re-present any aspect of the Allende extract in poetical form;*
d) *re-present any aspect of the Orwell extract in dramatic form.*

- *Notice which aspects of the text fare best in the transition to another format. Is 'realism' one of those aspects?*
- *How would your definition of realism fare with examples from television, poetry, theatre, diaries, newspapers, etc?*

BEYOND REALISM

You will need a clean sheet of paper by your side as you work. Read the following extracts and pay attention to the way your brain goes about making sense of the text. Observe your own reactions and *as you read*, jot down the impressions that pass through your mind such as images, questions and remarks. When you have finished reading give yourself a few minutes to reflect on each extract and write down your thoughts as they develop.

Your jotted notes are for your eyes only. Do not bother to write in full neat sentences. Reminder 'notes' are sufficient and will not slow you down.

1 riverrun, past Eve and Adam's, from swerve of shore to bend of bay, brings us by a commodius vicus of recirculation back to Howth Castle and Environs.

Sir Tristram, violer d'amores, fr'over the short sea, had passencore rearrived from North Armorica on this side the scraggy isthmus of Europe Minor to wielderfight his penisolate war: nor had topsawyer's rocks by the stream Oconee exaggerated themselse to Laurens County's gorgios while they went doublin their mumper all the time: nor avoice from afire bellowsed mishe mishe to tauftauf thuartpeatrick: not yet, though venissoon after, had a kidscad buttended a bland old isaac: not yet, though all's fair in vanessy, were sosie sesthers wroth with twone nathandjoe. Rot a peck of pa's malt had Jhem or Shen brewed by arclight and rory end to the regginbrow was to be seen ringsome on the aquaface.

The fall (bababadalgharaghtakamminarronnkonnbronntonnerronntuonn-thunntrovarrhounawnskawntoohoohoordenenthurnuk!) of a once wallstrait oldparr is retaled early in bed and later on life down through all christian minstrelsy. The great fall of the offwall entailed at such short notice the pftjschute of Finnegan, erse solid man, that the humptyhillhead of humself prumptly sends an unquiring one well to the west in quest of his tumptytum-toes: and their upturnpikepointandplace is at the knock out in the park where oranges have been laid to rust upon the green since devlinsfirst loved livvy.

(from *Finnegan's Wake* by James Joyce)

2   Palace in smoky light,
            Troy but a heap of smouldering boundary stones,
            ANAXIFORMINGES! Aurunculeia!
            Hear me. Cadmus of Golden Prows!
            The silver mirrors catch the bright stones and flare,
            Dawn, to our waking, drifts in the green cool light;
            Dew-haze blurs, in the grass, pale ankles moving.
            Beat, beat, whirr, thud, in the soft turf
                  under the apple trees,
            Choros nympharum, goat-foot, with the pale foot alternate;
            Crescent of blue-shot waters, green-gold in the shallows,
            A black cock crows in the sea-foam;

            And by the curved, carved foot of the couch,
                  claw-foot and lion head, an old man seated
            Speaking in the low drone . . . :
                  Ityn!
            Et ter flebiliter, Ityn Ityn!
            And she went toward the window and cast her down,
                  'All the while, the while, swallows crying:
            Ityn!
                  'It is Cabestan's heart in the dish.'
                  'It is Cabestan's heart in the dish?'
                  'No other taste shall change this.'
            And she went toward the window,
                  the slim white stone bar
            Making a double arch;
            Firm even fingers held to the firm pale stone:
            Swung for a moment,
                  and the wind out of Rhodez
            Caught in the full of her sleeve.
                . . . the swallows crying:
            'Tis. 'Tis. Ytis!
                Actaeon . . .
                and a valley,
            The valley is thick with leaves, with leaves, the trees,
            The sunlight glitters, glitters a-top,
            Like a fish-scale roof,
                Like the church roof in Poictiers
            If it were gold.
                      (from *Cantos* by Ezra Pound)

- *In a group, discuss your first reactions and the strategies you adopted to make sense of the extracts.*
- *What questions would you ask, and what further information would you seek to enhance your understanding?*
- *Notice what sort of information you expect in order to be able to unravel meaning.*
- *What positive reasons might the writers have had for choosing unconventional styles likely to surprise and even baffle their readers?*

MAKING MEANING

Writers run up against the edge of language all the time. They find that certain things are impossible to say, that meanings simply cannot be held within the language available. William Carlos Williams is one of many recent poets to make readers more aware of the limits of language and of the precarious nature of meaning. For example, his sequence of poems *Paintings From Breughel* nudges the reader out of complacency to consider the difficulties of communication itself. It is no accident that his poems look at the act of artistic creation, for the problems faced by poets are mirrored by the struggles of painters, sculptors, musicians and all artists to break through conventions to make new things sayable. In a sense, the following poem describes a difficulty which all artists and all audiences experience.

- *Read this poem and attempt a drawing of the picture it describes:*

SELF-PORTRAIT

In a red winter hat blue
eyes smiling
just the head and shoulders

crowded on the canvas
arms folded one
big ear the right showing

the face slightly tilted
a heavy wool coat
with broad buttons

gathered at the neck reveals
a bulbous nose
but the eyes red-rimmed

from over-use he must have
driven them hard
but the delicate wrists

show him to have been a
man unused to
manual labour unshaved his

blond beard half trimmed
no time for any-
thing but his painting

William Carlos Williams

- *Discuss the difficulties you had in reconstructing the picture from the poem, and pinpoint where these difficulties arise.*
- *What does your experience of reading the poem and drawing the picture suggest about the creative process in general? Do any of your conclusions also apply to writing?*

Whilst familiar forms can be reassuring, they also lead to complacency. Very often people learn to have limited tastes because they are intimidated by the unfamiliar. Understandably, all writers want to express their new awareness and very often this will mean finding a new form in which to express it.

READING BETWEEN THE LINES

What is *not* said in works of literature is as important as what *is* said. When we disagree with a writer, we are apt to notice evasions, tactical wordings and spurious arguments. Writers can make positive use of this impulse in readers to read between the lines by setting up deliberate 'gaps' which draw the reader in to speculate about the omissions. As the text progresses, these speculations may be revealed as misguided and the reader obliged to confront new ideas and challenge old assumptions.

What follows is a complete play by Samuel Beckett, the title of which – *Not I* – alerts the audience to its central concern. It has a powerful effect in the theatre and has been successfully produced as a television play starring Billie Whitelaw. If you cannot see or act it yourself, do sketch the set as it is described by Beckett. It has a significant visual impact.

- *You will need to read the play once alone, without a pause, to get the full impact of it. Then try going through it again more reflectively, allowing yourself time to pause and consider. Conduct the third reading in a small group, stopping at convenient points to speculate. You may find it useful to consider:*
  - *a) what we discover about Mouth's past, in particular the most recent traumatic experience;*
  - *b) what is represented by the auditor, in particular the attempts to gesture;*
  - *c) what the title of the play might mean.*

NOTE

Movement: this consists in simple sideways raising of arms from sides and their falling back, in a gesture of helpless compassion. It lessens with each recurrence till scarcely perceptible at third. There is just enough pause to contain it as MOUTH recovers from vehement refusal to relinquish third person.

Stage in darkness but for MOUTH, *upstage audience right, about 8 feet above stage level, faintly lit from close-up and below, rest of face in shadow. Invisible microphone.*
AUDITOR, *downstage audience left, tall standing figure, sex undeterminable, enveloped from head to foot in loose black djellaba, with hood, fully faintly lit, standing on invisible podium about 4 feet high shown by attitude alone to be facing diagonally across stage intent on* MOUTH, *dead still throughout but for four brief movements where indicated. See Note.*
As house lights down MOUTH's *voice unintelligible behind curtain. House lights out. Voice continues unintelligible behind curtain, 10 seconds. With rise of curtain ad-libbing from text as required leading when curtain fully up and attention sufficient into:*

MOUTH: . . . . out . . . into this world . . . this world . . . tiny little thing . . .
before its time . . . in a godfor– . . . what? . . girl? . . yes . . . tiny little girl
. . . into this . . . out into this . . . before her time . . . godforsaken hole
called . . . called . . . no matter . . . parents unknown . . . unheard of . . .
he having vanished . . . thin air . . . no sooner buttoned up his breeches
. . . she similarly . . . eight months later . . . almost to the tick . . . so no
love . . . spared that . . . no love such as normally vented on the . . .
speechless infant . . . in the home . . . no . . . nor indeed for that matter
any of any kind . . . no love of any kind . . . at any subsequent stage . . . so
typical affair . . . nothing of any note till coming up to sixty when– . . .
what? . . seventy? . . good God! . . coming up to seventy . . . wandering in
a field . . . looking aimlessly for cowslips . . . to make a ball . . . a few
steps then stop . . . stare into space . . . then on . . . a few more . . . stop
and stare again . . . so on . . . drifting around . . . when suddenly . . .
gradually . . . all went out . . . all that early April morning light . . . and
she found herself in the– . . . what? . . who? . . no! . . she! . . (*Pause and
movement 1.*) . . . found herself in the dark . . . and if not exactly . . .
insentient . . . insentient . . . for she could still hear the buzzing . . .
so-called . . . in the ears . . . and a ray of light came and went . . . came
and went . . . such as the moon might cast . . . drifting . . . in and out of
cloud . . . but so dulled . . . feeling . . . feeling so dulled . . . she did not
know . . . what position she was in . . . imagine! . . what position she was
in! . . whether standing . . . or sitting . . . but the brain– . . . what? . .
kneeling? . . yes . . . whether standing . . . or sitting . . . or kneeling . . .
but the brain– . . . what? . . lying? . . yes . . . whether standing . . . or
sitting . . . or kneeling . . . or lying . . . but the brain still . . . still . . . in a
way . . . for her first thought was . . . oh long after . . . sudden flash . . .
brought up as she had been to believe . . . with the other waifs . . . in a
merciful . . . (*Brief laugh.*) . . . God . . . (*Good laugh.*) . . . first thought was
. . . oh long after . . . sudden flash . . . she was being punished . . . for her
sins . . . a number of which then . . . further proof if proof were needed
. . . flashed through her mind . . . one after another . . . then dismissed
as foolish . . . oh long after . . . this thought dismissed . . . as she
suddenly realized . . . gradually realized . . . she was not suffering . . .
imagine! . . not suffering! . . indeed could not remember . . . off-hand
. . . when she had suffered less . . . unless of course she was . . . *meant* to
be suffering . . . ha! . . *thought* to be suffering . . . just as the odd time . . .

in her life . . . when clearly intended to be having pleasure . . . she was in
fact . . . having none . . . not the slightest . . . in which case of course . . .
that notion of punishment . . . for some sin or other . . . or for the lot . . .
or no particular reason . . . for its own sake . . . thing she understood
perfectly . . . that notion of punishment . . . which had first occurred to
her . . . brought up as she had been to believe . . . with the other waifs
. . . in a merciful . . . (*Brief laugh.*) . . . God . . . (*Good laugh.*) . . . first
occurred to her . . . then dismissed . . . as foolish . . . was perhaps not so
foolish . . . after all . . . so on . . . all that . . . vain reasonings . . . till
another thought . . . oh long after . . . sudden flash . . . very foolish really
but– . . . what? . . the buzzing? . . yes . . . all the time the buzzing . . .
so-called . . . in the ears . . . though of course actually . . . not in the ears
at all . . . in the skull . . . dull roar in the skull . . . and all the time this ray
or beam . . . like moonbeam . . . but probably not . . . certainly not . . .
always the same spot . . . now bright . . . now shrouded . . . but always
the same spot . . . as no moon could . . . no . . . no moon . . . just all part
of the same wish to . . . torment . . . though actually in point of fact . . .
not in the least . . . not a twinge . . . so far . . . ha! . . so far . . . this other
thought then . . . oh long after . . . sudden flash . . . very foolish really
but so like her . . . in a way . . . that she might do well to . . . groan . . . on
and off . . . writhe she could not . . . as if in actual agony . . . but could
not . . . could not bring herself . . . some flaw in her make-up . . .
incapable of deceit . . . or the machine . . . more likely the machine . . .
so disconnected . . . never got the message . . . or powerless to respond
. . . like numbed . . . couldn't make the sound . . . not any sound . . . no
sound of any kind . . . no screaming for help for example . . . should she
feel so inclined . . . scream . . . (*Screams.*) . . . then listen . . . (*Silence.*) . . .
scream again . . . (*Screams again.*) . . . then listen again . . . (*Silence.*) . . .
no . . . spared that . . . all silent as the grave . . . no part– . . . what? . . the
buzzing? . . yes . . . all silent but for the buzzing . . . so-called . . . no part
of her moving . . . that she could feel . . . just the eyelids . . . presumably
. . . on and off . . . shut out the light . . . reflex they call it . . . no feeling of
any kind . . . but the lids . . . even best of times . . . who feels them? . .
opening . . . shutting . . . all that moisture . . . but the brain still . . . still
sufficiently . . . oh very much so! . . at this stage . . . in control . . . under
control . . . to question even this . . . for on that April morning . . . so it
reasoned . . . that April morning . . . she fixing with her eye . . . a distant
bell . . . as she hastened towards it . . . fixing it with her eye . . . lest it
elude her . . . had not all gone out . . . all that light . . . of itself . . .
without any . . . any . . . on her part . . . so on . . . so on it reasoned . . .
vain questionings . . . and all dead still . . . sweet silent as the grave . . .
when suddenly . . . gradually . . . she realiz– . . . what? . . the buzzing? . .
yes . . . all dead still but for the buzzing . . . when suddenly she realized
. . . words were– . . . what? . . who? . . no! . . she! . . (*Pause and movement
2.*) . . . realized . . . words were coming . . . imagine! . . words were
coming . . . a voice she did not recognize . . . at first . . . so long since it
had sounded . . . then finally had to admit . . . could be none other . . .
than her own . . . certain vowel sounds . . . she had never heard . . .
elsewhere . . . so that people would stare . . . the rare occasions . . . once
or twice a year . . . always winter some strange reason . . . stare at her
uncomprehending . . . and now this stream . . . steady stream . . . she

who had never . . . on the contrary . . . practically speechless . . . all her
days . . . how she survived! . . even shopping . . . out shopping . . . busy
shopping centre . . . supermart . . . just hand in the list . . . with the bag
. . . old black shopping bag . . . then stand there waiting . . . any length of
time . . . middle of the throng . . . motionless . . . staring into space . . .
mouth half open as usual . . . till it was back in her hand . . . the bag back
in her hand . . . then pay and go . . . not as much as good-bye . . . how
she survived! . . and now this stream . . . not catching the half of it . . .
not the quarter . . . no idea . . . what she was saying . . . imagine! . . no
idea what she was saying! . . till she began trying to . . . delude herself
. . . it was not hers at all . . . not her voice at all . . . and no doubt would
have . . . vital she should . . . was on the point . . . after long efforts . . .
when suddenly she felt . . . gradually she felt . . . her lips moving . . .
imagine! . . her lips moving! . . as of course till then she had not . . . and
not alone the lips . . . the cheeks . . . the jaws . . . the whole face . . . all
those– . . . what? . . the tongue? . . yes . . . the tongue in the mouth . . . all
those contortions without which . . . no speech possible . . . and yet in
the ordinary way . . . not felt at all . . . so intent one is . . . on what one is
saying . . . the whole being . . . hanging on its words . . . so that not only
she had . . . had she . . . not only had she . . . to give up . . . admit hers
alone . . . her voice alone . . . but this other awful thought . . . oh long
after . . . sudden flash . . . even more awful if possible . . . that feeling
was coming back . . . imagine! . . feeling coming back! . . starting at the
top . . . then working down . . . the whole machine . . . but no . . . spared
that . . . the mouth alone . . . so far . . . ha! . . so far . . . then thinking . . .
oh long after . . . sudden flash . . . it can't go on . . . all this . . . all that . . .
steady stream . . . straining to hear . . . make something of it . . . and her
own thoughts . . . make something of them . . . all– . . . what? . . the
buzzing? . . yes . . . all the time the buzzing . . . so-called . . . all that
together . . . imagine! . . whole body like gone . . . just the mouth . . . lips
. . . cheeks . . . jaws . . . never– . . . what? . . tongue? . . yes . . . lips . . .
cheeks . . . jaws . . . tongue . . . never still a second . . . mouth on fire . . .
stream of words . . . in her ear . . . practically in her ear . . . not catching
the half . . . not the quarter . . . no idea what she's saying . . . imagine! . .
no idea what she's saying! . . and can't stop . . . no stopping it . . . she
who but a moment before . . . but a moment! . . could not make a sound
. . . no sound of any kind . . . now can't stop . . . imagine! . . can't stop
the stream . . . and the whole brain begging . . . something begging in
the brain . . . begging the mouth to stop . . . pause a moment . . . if only
for a moment . . . and no response . . . as if it hadn't heard . . . or
couldn't . . . couldn't pause a second . . . like maddened . . . all that
together . . . straining to hear . . . piece it together . . . and the brain . . .
raving away on its own . . . trying to make sense of it . . . or make it stop
. . . or in the past . . . dragging up the past . . . flashes from all over . . .
walks mostly . . . walking all her days . . . day after day . . . a few steps
then stop . . . stare into space . . . then on . . . a few more . . . stop and
stare again . . . so on . . . drifting around . . . day after day . . . or that
time she cried . . . the one time she could remember . . . since she was a
baby . . . must have cried as a baby . . . perhaps not . . . not essential to
life . . . just the birth cry to get her going . . . breathing . . . then no more
till this . . . old hag already . . . sitting staring at her hand . . . where was

it? . . Croker's Acres . . . one evening on the way home . . . home! . . a
little mound in Croker's Acres . . . dusk . . . sitting staring at her hand
. . . there in her lap . . . palm upward . . . suddenly saw it wet . . . the
palm . . . tears presumably . . . hers presumably . . . no one else for miles
. . . no sound . . . just the tears . . . sat and watched them dry . . . all over
in a second . . . or grabbing at straw . . . the brain . . . flickering away on
its own . . . quick grab and on . . . nothing there . . . on to the next . . .
bad as the voice . . . worse . . . as little sense . . . all that together . . .
can't– . . . what? . . the buzzing? . . yes . . . all the time the buzzing . . .
dull roar like falls . . . and the beam . . . flickering on and off . . . starting
to move around . . . like moonbeam but not . . . all part of the same . . .
keep an eye on that too . . . corner of the eye . . . all that together . . .
can't go on . . . God is love . . . she'll be purged . . . back in the field . . .
morning sun . . . April . . . sink face down in the grass . . . nothing but
the larks . . . so on . . . grabbing at the straw . . . straining to hear . . . the
odd word . . . make some sense of it . . . whole body like gone . . . just
the mouth . . . like maddened . . . and can't stop . . . no stopping it . . .
something she– . . . something she had to– . . . what? . . who? . . no! . .
she! . . (*Pause and movement 3.*) . . . something she had to– . . . what? . .
the buzzing? . . yes . . . all the time the buzzing . . . dull roar . . . in the
skull . . . and the beam . . . ferreting around . . . painless . . . so far . . .
ha! . . so far . . . then thinking . . . oh long after . . . sudden flash . . .
perhaps something she had to . . . had to . . . tell . . . could that be it? . .
something she had to . . . tell . . . tiny little thing . . . before its time . . .
godforsaken hole . . . no love . . . spared that . . . speechless all her days
. . . practically speechless . . . how she survived! . . that time in court . . .
what had she to say for herself . . . guilty or not guilty . . . stand up
woman . . . speak up woman . . . stood there staring into space . . .
mouth half open as usual . . . waiting to be led away . . . glad of the hand
on her arm . . . now this . . . something she had to tell . . . could that be
it? . . something that would tell . . . how it was . . . how she– . . . what? . .
had been? . . yes . . . something that would tell how it had been . . . how
she had lived . . . lived on and on . . . guilty or not . . . on and on . . . to be
sixty . . . something she– . . . what? . . seventy? . . good God! . . on and on
to be seventy . . . something she didn't know herself . . . wouldn't know
if she heard . . . then forgiven . . . God is love . . . tender mercies . . . new
every morning . . . back in the field . . . April morning . . . face in the
grass . . . nothing but the larks . . . pick it up there . . . get on with it from
there . . . another few– . . . what? . . not that? . . nothing to do with that?
. . nothing she could tell? . . all right . . . nothing she could tell . . . try
something else . . . think of something else . . . oh long after . . . sudden
flash . . . not that either . . . all right . . . something else again . . . so on
. . . hit on it in the end . . . think everything keep on long enough . . .
then forgiven . . . back in the– . . . what? . . not that either? . . nothing to
do with that either? . . nothing she could think? . . all right . . . nothing
she could tell . . . nothing she could think . . . nothing she– . . . what? . .
who? . . no! . . she! . . (*Pause and movement 4.*) . . . tiny little thing . . . out
before its time . . . godforsaken hole . . . no love . . . spared that . . .
speechless all her days . . . practically speechless . . . even to herself . . .
never out loud . . . but not completely . . . sometimes sudden urge . . .
once or twice a year . . . always winter some strange reason . . . the long

evenings . . . hours of darkness . . . sudden urge to . . . tell . . . then rush
out stop the first she saw . . . nearest lavatory . . . start pouring it out . . .
steady stream . . . mad stuff . . . half the vowels wrong . . . no one could
follow . . . till she saw the stare she was getting . . . then die of shame . . .
crawl back in . . . once or twice a year . . . always winter some strange
reason . . . long hours of darkness . . . now this . . . this . . . quicker and
quicker . . . the words . . . the brain . . . flickering away like mad . . .
quick grab and on . . . nothing there . . . on somewhere else . . . try
somewhere else . . . all the time something begging . . . something in her
begging . . . begging it all to stop . . . unanswered . . . prayer unanswered
. . . or unheard . . . too faint . . . so on . . . keep on . . . trying . . . not
knowing what . . . what she was trying . . . what to try . . . whole body like
gone . . . just the mouth . . . like maddened . . . so on . . . keep– . . . what?
. . the buzzing? . . yes . . . all the time the buzzing . . . dull roar like falls
. . . in the skull . . . and the beam . . . poking around . . . painless . . . so
far . . . ha! . . so far . . . all that . . . keep on . . . not knowing what . . .
what she was– . . . what? . . who? . . no! . . she! . . SHE! . . (*Pause.*) . . .
what she was trying . . . what to try . . . no matter . . . keep on . . .
(*Curtain starts down.*) . . . hit on it in the end . . . then back . . . God is
love . . . tender mercies . . . new every morning . . . back in the field . . .
April morning . . . face in the grass . . . nothing but the larks . . . pick it
up –

(*Curtain fully down. House dark. Voice continues behind curtain,
unintelligible, 10 seconds, ceases as house lights up.*)

Plays like *Not I* defy a definitive interpretation: that is part of their
purpose. You may find it useful to consider the way the play speculates
with ideas about the nature of identity and the function of language.

- *Sum up your reactions to the play by reporting back on:*
    a) its general impact on the group;
    b) the difficulties which confronted you in making sense of it;
    *c) how such difficulties might provoke constructive thought on the part of
    an audience;*
    d) what reflections the play might prompt about communication;
    *e) what the play suggests about the relationship between our use of
    language and our identity.*

Reading List

Magical realism (refer to page 92): Salman Rushdie's *Midnight's
Children* (Jonathan Cape, 1981) is an example from a writer with an
Asian background writing in English. Isabel Allende of Chile is quoted
in this chapter – try *The House of the Spirits* (Jonathan Cape, 1985). The
stories of Jorge Luis Borges, another Latin American writer, defy a
label, but the anthology *Fictions* (John Calder, 1985) contains his best,
most tantalising stories. We have enjoyed *One Hundred Years of Solitude*
by Gabriel Garcia Marquez (Picador, 1978). An English writer whose

work comes close to this tradition is Angela Carter – try *The Magic Toyshop* (Virago, 1981).

Much twentieth century literature flirts with the edge of meaning, but the public imagination has been arrested by examples from art. A taste for 'isms' will guide you to the appropriate people: surrealism, cubism, vorticism, constructivism, modernism and so on. These movements had an impact on all the arts, including literature. Because these movements are breaking away from the dominant traditions, the texts can be daunting to read; but you should look over them with an open mind and persevere a little.

Poetry offers obvious examples: T. S. Eliot's *The Waste Land* (Macmillan, 1968) is essential reading: it dropped like a bomb on the landscape of English Literature. American poets such as Wallace Stevens, Hart Crane and William Carlos Williams broke new ground in their efforts to achieve an un-English identity.

Drama offers particularly striking examples of literature drawing attention to its own artifice: Beckett, Pinter, Stoppard and Pirandello are essential reading.

Novelists have also been preoccupied with their own art. Some recent popular works include the novels of John Fowles, for example *The French Lieutenant's Woman* (Jonathan Cape, 1969). Umberto Eco is a dense but interesting writer and *The Name of the Rose* (Picador, 1986) is readily available. *If On a Winter's Night A Traveller* by Italo Calvino (Picador, 1982) is a clever novel about the processes of reading, writing and creativity. An older but important work is *Finnegan's Wake* by James Joyce (Faber and Faber, 1975). It is extraordinarily demanding, but take a look at it.

It is not only during the twentieth century that work has been taking place at the edge of meaning; writers have been breaking moulds for centuries, and writing about the artifice of language. Laurence Sterne's *The Life and Opinions of Tristram Shandy* (Oxford University Press, 1983) is an obvious example.

TEXT PLAY

TEXTS WHICH TALK ABOUT THEMSELVES

The following extract is from John Fowles's novel, *The French Lieutenant's Woman*, a story set in the nineteenth century and one which questions the possibilities of writing a realist novel in the 1960s. Read the passage, which interrupts a conventional narrative, and consider the issues it raises about the creation of fiction:

For the drift of the Maker is dark, an Isis hid by the veil . . .

Tennyson, *Maud* (1855)

I do not know. This story I am telling is all imagination. These characters I create never existed outside my own mind. If I have pretended until now to know my characters' minds and innermost thoughts, it is because I am writing in (just as I have assumed some of the vocabulary and 'voice' of) a convention universally accepted at the time of my story: that the novelist stands next to God. He may not know all, yet he tries to pretend that he does. But I live in the age of Alain Robbe-Grillet and Roland Barthes; if this is a novel, it cannot be a novel in the modern sense of the word. [. . .]

Perhaps you suppose that a novelist has only to pull the right strings and his puppets will behave in a lifelike manner; and produce on request a thorough analysis of their motives and intentions. Certainly I intended at this stage (*Chap. Thirteen – unfolding of Sarah's true state of mind*) to tell all – or all that matters. But I find myself suddenly like a man in the sharp spring night, watching from the lawn beneath that dim upper window in Marlborough House; I know in the context of my book's reality that Sarah would never have brushed away her tears and leant down and delivered a chapter of revelation. She would instantly have turned, had she seen me there just as the old moon rose, and disappeared into the interior shadows.

But I am a novelist, not a man in a garden – I can follow her where I like. But possibility is not permissibility. Husbands could often murder their wives – and the reverse – and get away with it. But they don't. [. . .]

In other words, to be free myself, I must give him, and Tina, and Sarah, even the abominable Mrs Poulteney, their freedoms as well. There is only one good definition of God: the freedom that allows other freedoms to exist. And I must conform to that definition.

The novelist is still a god, since he creates (and not even the most aleatory avant-garde modern novel has managed to extirpate its author completely); what has changed is that we are no longer the gods of the Victorian image, omniscient and decreeing; but in the new theological image, with freedom our first principle, not authority.

(from *The French Lieutenant's Woman* by John Fowles)

- *What questions about writing fiction are raised here?*
- *What purposes might a writer have in breaking with the narrative in this way?*
- *What effect does this have on the reader?*

The appeal of narrative is such that even in this century much fiction continues in the realist mode, the novel posing itself as an accurate reflection of the world into which it has invited its reader. But many writers have turned the mirror on the act of writing instead: they deliberately focus the reader's attention on the construction of the text and break the illusions of the fictional world. The reader cannot escape the understanding that the text is an artefact, and is obliged to consider not only the relationship of fiction to reality, but also the possibility that what we see as the 'real world' of historical events is also open to question: if a world can be made up, can be a figment of the imagination, then why not *the* world? In a similar way, if Napoleon or Freud are just 'other' characters in books (as they are in the novels *The Passion* and *The White Hotel* respectively: see the reading list) then the distinctions between fiction and fact, history and story become blurred.

Just as there are ways in which a text can use techniques to conceal its production and convince the reader of its authority as a mirror on the world, there are also many ways in which a text can draw attention to itself *as a text*.

The following are examples from the eighteenth and twentieth centuries:

I   CHAPTER THIRTY-EIGHT

To conceive this right, – call for pen and ink – here's paper ready to your hand. – Sit down, Sir, paint her to your own mind – as like your mistress as you can – as unlike your wife as your conscience will let you – 'tis all one to me – please but your own fancy in it.

—Was ever any thing in Nature so sweet – so exquisite!

– Then, dear Sir, how could my uncle Toby resist it?

Thrice happy book! thou wilt have one page, at least, within thy covers, which MALICE will not blacken and which IGNORANCE cannot misrepresent.

CHAPTER FORTY

I AM now beginning to get fairly into my work; and by the help of a vegitable diet, with a few of the cold seeds, I make no doubt but I shall be able to go on with my uncle Toby's story, and my own, in a tolerable straight line. Now,

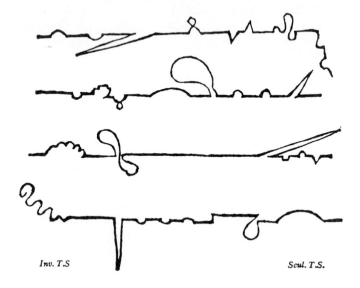

Inv. T.S   *Scul. T.S.*

These were the four lines I moved in through my first, second, third, and fourth volumes. – In the fifth volume I have been very good, – the precise line I have described in it being this:

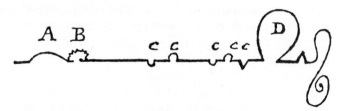

By which it appears, that except at the curve, marked A. where I took a trip to Navarre, – and the indented curve B. which is the short airing when I was there with the Lady Baussiere and her page, – I have not taken the least frisk of a digression, till John de la Casse's devils led me the round you see marked D. – for as for *cccc* they are nothing but parentheses, and the common *ins* and *outs* incident to the lives of the greatest ministers of state; and when compared with what men have done, – or with my own transgressions at the letters A B D – they vanish into nothing.

In this last volume I have done better still – for from the end of Le Fever's episode, to the beginning of my uncle Toby's campaigns, – I have scarce stepped a yard out of my way.

If I mend at this rate, it is not impossible – by the good leave of his grace of Benevento's devils – but I may arrive hereafter at the excellency of going on even thus;

which is a line drawn as straight as I could draw it, by a writing-master's ruler, (borrowed for that purpose) turning neither to the right hand or to the left.

This *right line*, – the path-way for Christians to walk in! say divines –

– The emblem of moral rectitude! says Cicero –

– The *best line*! say cabbage planters – is the shortest line says Archimedes, which can be drawn from one given point to another. –

I wish your ladyships would lay this matter to heart, in your next birth-day suits!

– What a journey!

Pray can you tell me, – that is, without anger, before I write my chapter upon straight lines – by what mistake – who told them so – or how it has come to pass, that your men of wit and genius have all along confounded this line, with the line of GRAVITATION?

(from *Tristram Shandy* by Laurence Sterne)

2 PRODUCER: (*At first utterly astonished and then indignant.*) Shut up! What the . . . ! (*Then turning to the* CHARACTERS.) And you get out of here! Clear out of here! (*To the* STAGE-MANAGER.) For God's sake, clear them out!

STAGE-MANAGER: (*Coming forward, but then stopping as if held back by some strange dismay.*) Go away! Go away!

FATHER: (*To the* PRODUCER.) No, no! Listen. . . We. . .

PRODUCER: (*Shouting.*) I tell you, we've got work to do!

LEADING MAN: You can't go about playing practical jokes like this. . .

FATHER: (*Resolutely coming forward.*) I wonder at your incredulity. Is it perhaps that you're not accustomed to seeing the characters created by an author leaping to life up here on the stage, when they come face to face with each other? Or is it, perhaps, that there's no script there (*He points to the prompt box*) that contains us?

STEPDAUGHTER: (*Smiling, she steps towards the* PRODUCER; *then, in a wheedling voice.*) Believe me, sir, we really are six characters . . . and very, very interesting! But we've been cut adrift.

FATHER: (*Brushing her aside.*) Yes, that's it, we've been cut adrift. (*And then immediately to the* PRODUCER.) In the sense, you understand, that the author who created us as living beings, either couldn't or wouldn't put us materially into the world of art. And it was truly a crime . . . because he who has the good fortune to be born a living character may snap his fingers at Death even. He will never die! Man . . . The writer . . . The instrument of creation . . . Will die. . . . But what is created by him will never die. And in order to live eternally he has not the slightest need of extraordinary gifts or of accomplishing prodigies. Who was Sancho Panza? Who was Don Abbondio? And yet they live eternally because – living seeds – they had the good fortune to find a fruitful womb – a fantasy which knew how to raise and nourish them, and to make them live through all eternity.

PRODUCER: All this is very, very fine indeed. . . . But what do you want here?
FATHER: We wish to live, sir!
PRODUCER: (*Ironically.*) Through all eternity?
FATHER: No, sir; just for a moment . . . in you.
AN ACTOR: Listen to him! . . . listen to him!
LEADING LADY: They want to live in us!
JUVENILE LEAD: (*Pointing to the* STEPDAUGHTER.) I've no objection . . . so
    long as I get her.
FATHER: Listen! Listen! The play is in the making. (*To the* PRODUCER.) But
    if you and your actors are willing, we can settle it all between us without
    further delay.
PRODUCER: (*Annoyed.*) But what do you want to settle? We don't go in for
    that sort of concoction here! We put on comedies and dramas here.
FATHER: Exactly! That's the very reason why we came to you.
PRODUCER: And where's the script?
FATHER: It is in us, sir. (*The* ACTORS *laugh.*) The drama is in us. *We* are the
    drama and we are impatient to act it – so fiercely does our inner passion
    urge us on.

(from *Six Characters in Search of an Author* by Luigi Pirandello)

3 'Excuse me,' he said, moving back to face Karl, who had gone pale as a
sheet. 'You can put your hands down now,' said the sheriff, flushing down to
the opening in his shirt. 'There seems to have been a mistake.'

There was a long moment of tension. I looked at each of the men
carefully. They looked carefully at me.

'It's true,' I finally said. 'Let me fetch the book.'

'I think there has been a mistake,' Sheriff Pausch repeated, and just that
suddenly, because there was a wary gentleness in his voice, I knew that I had
done something very wrong. Worse yet, I knew that something even more
wrong was going to happen. I looked down at Karl. The legs of his chair had
sunk still farther.

'Stop . . . that,' I slowly commanded.

'Sita, sit down now, please,' said Louis.

But I was locked in an upright position by Karl's dark strained stare. I
could not take my eyes away although I had to bend across the table to see
him clearly, he'd sunk so far. The air was very still. The tiny birds, light as
moths, hovered in the trumpet flowers. One note sounded. I meant to ask
Louis if he heard it as well. But then my cousin leaned over sideways and
pulled the heavy-looking case, the one he'd dragged through the clematis,
onto his lap. He sat there with the case clasped in his arms, perhaps
intending to open it, perhaps intending to go. Instead, something happened.

The case was so heavy, resting on his lap and knees, that his feet began to
bury themselves in the earth and very swiftly the lawn rose to his knees. I said
nothing. I was paralyzed with fear. I had betrayed him and now I could only
watch as the man, the chair, continued to sink. The case submerged. The
lawn crept up his oxblood shirt. The grass brushed his chin. And still he
continued to go down.

It is too late, I thought, watching him, unless he says the healing words.

'Mea culpa,' I gasped. *'Mea maxima culpa.'*

But already his mouth was sealed by earth. His ears were stopped. His mild, sad eyes were covered and then there was only the pale strip of his forehead. The earth paused before swallowing him entirely, and then, quite suddenly, the rest of him went under. The last I saw was the careless white cross in his oiled hair. The ground shook slightly to cover him, and there was nothing where he had been.

(from The Beet Queen by Louise Erdrich)

- *In what ways does each of these extracts point to its own construction?*
- *In what way can the interruption of 'realism' affect the way writers write and readers read fiction? Are there any dangers or limitations for writers using such techniques?*
- *The film of* The French Lieutenant's Woman *reproduces the self-references in the novel by cutting in a story about the actors in the film. Can you think of examples from other media, such as art, film, television or advertising, which refer to their own production? How do they work?*

BORROWING THE TEXT

Some texts, or features from a text do become widely known, part of a common source of reference: few people would not understand a reference to Romeo, even if they did not know Shakespeare's play. These fictions make such an impression that we may speculate about their continuation in another context.

Two characters transported in this way are Rosencrantz and Guildenstern, friends of Hamlet in Shakespeare's play. They are summoned to court by the King, Claudius (Hamlet's new stepfather and murderer of his father), in order to gain his confidence and reveal what he is thinking. These minor characters are given their own play in Tom Stoppard's *Rosencrantz and Guildenstern Are Dead*, written in 1968:

1 HAMLET: What news?
ROSENCRANTZ: None, my lord, but that the world's grown honest.
HAMLET: Then is doomsday near. But your news is not true. Let me question more in particular. What have you, my good friends, deserved at the hands of Fortune that she sends you to prison hither?
GUILDENSTERN: Prison, my lord?
HAMLET: Denmark's a prison.
ROSENCRANTZ: Then is the world one.
HAMLET: A goodly one, in which there are many confines, wards, and dungeons, Denmark being one o' th' worst.
ROSENCRANTZ: We think not so, my lord.
HAMLET: Why, then 'tis none to you, for there is nothing either good or bad but thinking makes it so. To me it is a prison.
ROSENCRANTZ: Why then your ambition makes it one. 'Tis too narrow for your mind.
HAMLET: O God, I could be bounded in a nutshell and count myself a king of infinite space, were it not that I have bad dreams.

GUILDENSTERN: Which dreams indeed are ambition, for the very substance of the ambitious is merely the shadow of a dream.

HAMLET: A dream itself is but a shadow.

ROSENCRANTZ: Truly, and I hold ambition of so airy and light a quality that it is but a shadow's shadow.

HAMLET: Then are our beggars bodies, and our monarchs and outstretched heroes the beggars' shadows. Shall we to th' court? For, by my fay, I cannot reason.

BOTH: We'll wait upon you.

HAMLET: No such matter. I will not sort you with the rest of my servants, for, to speak to you like an honest man, I am most dreadfully attended. But in the beaten way of friendship, what make you at Elsinore?

ROSENCRANTZ: To visit you, my lord; no other occasion.

HAMLET: Beggar that I am, I am even poor in thanks, but I thank you; and sure, dear friends, my thanks are too dear a halfpenny. Were you not sent for? Is it your own inclining? Is it a free visitation? Come, come, deal justly with me. Come, come; nay, speak.

GUILDENSTERN: What should we say, my lord?

HAMLET: Why anything – but to th' purpose. You were sent for, and there is a kind of confession in your looks, which your modesties have not craft enough to colour. I know the good King and Queen have sent for you.

ROSENCRANTZ: To what end, my lord?

HAMLET: That you must teach me. But let me conjure you by the rights of our fellowship, by the consonancy of our youth, by the obligation of our ever-preserved love, and by what more dear a better proposer can charge you withal, be even and direct with me, whether you were sent for or no.

ROSENCRANTZ: (*Aside to* GUILDENSTERN.) What say you?

HAMLET: (*Aside.*) Nay then, I have an eye of you. – If you love me, hold not off.

GUILDENSTERN: My lord, we were sent for.

HAMLET: I will tell you why; so shall my anticipation prevent your discovery, and your secrecy to the King and Queen molt no feather. I have of late, but wherefore I know not, lost all my mirth, forgone all custom of exercises; and indeed, it goes so heavily with my disposition that this goodly frame, the earth, seems to me a sterile promontory; this most excellent canopy, the air, look you, this brave o'erhanging firmament, this majestical roof fretted with golden fire: why, it appeareth nothing to me but a foul and pestilent congregation of vapors. What a piece of work is a man, how noble in reason, how infinite in faculties, in form and moving how express and admirable, in action how like an angel, in apprehension how like a god: the beauty of the world, the paragon of animals; and yet to me, what is this quintessence of dust? Man delights not me; nor woman neither, though by your smiling you seem to say so.

ROSENCRANTZ: My lord, there was no such stuff in my thoughts.

HAMLET: Why did ye laugh then, when I said 'Man delights not me'?

ROSENCRANTZ: To think, my lord, if you delight not in man, what lenten entertainment the players shall receive from you. We coted them on the way, and hither are they coming to offer you service.

(from *Hamlet* by William Shakespeare)

2 (ROS *and* GUIL *ponder. Each reluctant to speak first.*)
GUIL: Hm?
ROS: Yes?
GUIL: What?
ROS: I thought you. . . .
GUIL: No.
ROS: Ah.
(*Pause.*)
GUIL: I think we can say we made some headway.
ROS: You think so?
GUIL: I think we can say that.
ROS: I think we can say he made us look ridiculous.
GUIL: We played it close to the chest of course.
ROS (*Derisively*): 'Question and answer. Old ways are the best ways'! He was
scoring off us all down the line.
GUIL: He caught us on the wrong foot once or twice, perhaps, but I thought
we gained some ground.
ROS (*Simply*): He murdered us.
GUIL: He might have had the edge.
ROS (*Roused*): Twenty-seven – three, and you think he might have had the
edge?! He *murdered* us.
GUIL: What about our evasions?
ROS: Oh, our evasions were lovely. 'Were you sent for?' he says. 'My lord, we
were sent for . . .' I didn't know where to put myself.
GUIL: He had six rhetoricals—
ROS: It was question and answer, all right. Twenty-seven questions he got
out in ten minutes, and answered three. I was waiting for you to *delve*.
'When is he going to start *delving*?' I asked myself.
GUIL: – And two repetitions.
ROS: Hardly a leading question between us.
GUIL: We got his *symptoms*, didn't we?
ROS: Half of what he said meant something else, and the other half didn't
mean anything at all.
GUIL: Thwarted ambition – a sense of grievance, that's my diagnosis.
ROS: Six rhetorical and two repetition, leaving nineteen of which we
answered fifteen. And what did we get in return? He's depressed! . . .
Denmark's a prison and he'd rather live in a nutshell; some shadow-
play about the nature of ambition, which never got down to cases, and
finally one direct question which might have led somewhere, and led in
fact to his illuminating claim to tell a hawk from a handsaw.

(from *Rosencrantz and Guildenstern Are Dead* by Tom Stoppard)

● *Describe the relationship between the two plays as demonstrated in these
extracts.*
● *What insights or alternatives does Stoppard's play offer on Shakespeare's
play?*
● *Could Stoppard's play exist without Shakespeare's – does it matter if the
reader is unfamiliar with* Hamlet?

Other writers have 'answered back' for characters not centrally

placed in their original novel. For example, Jean Rhys in *Wide Sargasso
Sea* retells the story of Mr Rochester's first wife (the madwoman in
Charlotte Brontë's *Jane Eyre*), giving her version of the failure of the
relationship and her explanation of the 'madness'. Such an approach
can cast an unusual light on the original work.

● *Read the following poem, a monologue spoken by 'the Duke'. Then write the
story as seen by the Duchess, adopting the voice you consider appropriate.
You may try this in poetry or prose. The blank verse used by Browning is
considered a poetic form particularly suited to creating the effect of the
spoken voice.*

MY LAST DUCHESS

Ferrara

THAT's my last Duchess painted on the wall,
Looking as if she were alive. I call
That piece a wonder, now: Frà Pandolf's hands
Worked busily a day, and there she stands.
Will't please you sit and look at her? I said
'Frà Pandolf' by design, for never read
Strangers like you that pictured countenance,
The depth and passion of its earnest glance,
But to myself they turned (since none puts by
The curtain I have drawn for you, but I)
And seemed as they would ask me, if they durst,
How such a glance came there; so, not the first
Are you to turn and ask thus. Sir, 'twas not
Her husband's presence only, called that spot
Of joy into the Duchess' cheek: perhaps
Frà Pandolf chanced to say 'Her mantle laps
Over my lady's wrist too much,' or 'Paint
Must never hope to reproduce the faint
Half-flush that dies along her throat:' such stuff
Was courtesy, she thought, and cause enough
For calling up that spot of joy. She had
A heart – how shall I say? – too soon made glad,
Too easily impressed; she liked whate'er
She looked on, and her looks went everywhere.
Sir, 'twas all one! My favour at her breast,
The dropping of the daylight in the West,
The bough of cherries some officious fool
Broke in the orchard for her, the white mule
She rode with round the terrace – all and each
Would draw from her alike the approving speech,
Or blush, at least. She thanked men, – good! but thanked
Somehow – I know not how – as if she ranked
My gift of a nine-hundred-years-old name
With anybody's gift. Who'd stoop to blame
This sort of trifling? Even had you skill

In speech – (which I have not) – to make your will
Quite clear to such an one, and say, 'Just this
Or that in you disgusts me; here you miss,
Or there exceed the mark' – and if she let
Herself be lessoned so, nor plainly set
Her wits to yours, forsooth, and made excuse,
– E'en then would be some stooping; and I choose
Never to stoop. Oh sir, she smiled, no doubt,
Whene'er I passed her; but who passed without
Much the same smile? This grew; I gave commands;
Then all smiles stopped together. There she stands
As if alive. Will't please you rise? We'll meet
The company below, then. I repeat,
The Count your master's known munificence
Is ample warrant that no just pretence
Of mine for dowry will be disallowed;
Though his fair daughter's self, as I avowed
At starting, is my object. Nay, we'll go
Together down, sir. Notice Neptune, though,
Taming a sea-horse, thought a rarity,
Which Claus of Innsbruck cast in bronze for me!

Robert Browning

- *How far does your version of the Duchess' monologue depend upon and
develop the original?*

PARODY

When we consider a famous text we may bring to our reading
ready-formed ideas about the work. Read the poem below and discuss
your reactions to it:

I WANDERED LONELY AS A CLOUD

I wandered lonely as a Cloud
That floats on high o'er vales and hills,
When all at once I saw a crowd,
A host of golden Daffodils;
Beside the Lake, beneath the trees,
Fluttering and dancing in the breeze.

Continuous as the stars that shine
And twinkle on the milky way,
They stretched in never-ending line
Along the margin of a bay;
Ten thousand saw I at a glance,
Tossing their heads in sprightly dance.

The waves beside them danced but they
Out-did the sparkling waves in glee: –
A poet could not but be gay,
In such a jocund company;
I gazed – and gazed – but little thought
What wealth the show to me had
    brought:

For oft, when on my couch I lie
In vacant or in pensive mood,
They flash upon that inward eye
Which is the bliss of solitude,
And then my heart with pleasure fills,
And dances with the daffodils.

William Wordsworth

- *How far do the language and form of the poem meet your expectations of poetry?*
- *How far is your view of this poem affected by any previous knowledge you may have had of this verse or of the poet Wordsworth?*
- *What attitudes to poetry and to the poet are suggested in the poem?*
- *Consider the following treatments of the same poem. What aspects of the original text seem to be targeted and what views of poetry are implied?*

I   THE WORDSWORTHS

We wondered – nay, we said out loud,
'Oh happy, happy daffodils!'
Alas, but we had not allowed
For Him who haunts these gloomy hills,
His muffler flapping in the breeze,
Muttering and stumbling through the trees.

Lugubrious as the sheep that pine
And sulk behind each boulder damp,
He stands, disconsolate, for a time,
Underneath his dripping gamp.
While all about the rain drops fall;
We wish to God he wouldn't call.

We wish to hell he'd wander on,
We've never been so sorely tried.
A daffodil thus gazed upon,
Might well consider suicide.
He stares and stares, 'How rude!' We sing,
'What blank despair to us you bring.'

For oft, as in this bog we lie,
In vacant or in pensive mood,

He looms upon that inward eye,
Which is the curse of solitude;
And then our hearts of pleasure drain,
To see that dreary bard again.

William Bealby Wright

2   *The New, Fast, Automatic Daffodils*
    (New variation on Wordsworth's 'Daffodils')

I wandered lonely as
THE NEW, FAST DAFFODIL
    FULLY AUTOMATIC
that floats on high o'er vales and hills
The Daffodil is generous dimensioned to accommodate four adult
    passengers
10,000 saw I at a glance
Nodding their new anatomically shaped heads in sprightly dance
Beside the lake beneath the trees
    in three bright modern colours
red, blue and pigskin
The Daffodil de luxe is equipped with a host of useful accessories
including windscreen wiper and washer with joint control
A Daffodil doubles the enjoyment of touring at home or abroad

in vacant or in pensive mood
SPECIFICATION:
    Overall width   1·44m (57″)
    Overall height   1·38m (54·3″)
    Max. speed   105 km/hr (65m.p.h.)
        (also cruising speed)

DAFFODIL
    RELIABLE – ECONOMICAL
DAFFODIL
    THE BLISS OF SOLITUDE
DAFFODIL
    The Variomatic Inward Eye
Travelling by Daffodil you can relax and enjoy every mile of the journey.

(Cut-up of Wordsworth's poem plus Dutch motor-car leaflet)

Adrian Henri

● *Consider the following poem and the picture on page 117 and their parodies:*

1   ANTHEM FOR DOOMED YOUTH

What passing-bells for these who die as cattle?
    – Only the monstrous anger of the guns.
    Only the stuttering rifles' rapid rattle
Can patter out their hasty orisons.

No mockeries now for them; no prayers nor bells;
　　Nor any voice of mourning save the choirs, –
The shrill, demented choirs of wailing shells;
　　And bugles calling for them from sad shires.

What candles may be held to speed them all?
　　Not in the hands of boys, but in their eyes
Shall shine the holy glimmers of goodbyes.
　　The pallor of girls' brows shall be their pall;
Their flowers the tenderness of patient minds,
And each slow dusk a drawing-down of blinds.

Wilfred Owen

2   A THIRD WORLD WAR POEM

What passing words for these stacked up as chattels?
　　– Only the silence of ten searing suns.
　　– Only the muttering wireless' chat of battles
Is stammering out some sum of megatons.
No saccharine speech – they have no hair, no balls,
　　Nor had they word of warning, just the fires,
　　The whirling, white-hot fires which melted walls;
Now shovels shift some bits for massive pyres.

What petrol may be found to burn them all?
　　Not from the North Sea fields shall come the gas
To brighten up the last appalling Mass.
　　The acid, crass old lies are now their gall;
Their only trace shall be some blackened rind;
Their last trump one charred fart from God's behind.

Bill Greenwell

- *What relationships exist between*
  a) the original poem and its parody?
  b) the picture opposite and its parody?
- *After considering these and other examples, try to produce a definition of*
  parody.

(*The Peasant Wedding* by Breughel)

(from *Asterix in Belgium* by Goscinny & Uderzo)

Reading List

Texts which talk about themselves:
The French Lieutenant's Woman, John Fowles (Jonathan Cape, 1969)
Labyrinths, Jorge Luis Borges (Penguin, 1964)
Slaughterhouse Five, Kurt Vonnegut (Jonathan Cape, 1970)
Tristram Shandy, Laurence Sterne (Oxford University Press, 1983)

For drama try:
Six Characters in Search of an Author, Luigi Pirandello (Eyre Methuen, 1979)
The Real Inspector Hound, Tom Stoppard (Faber and Faber, 1970)
Waiting for Godot (Faber and Faber, 1956) or *Endgame* (Faber and Faber, 1964) both by Samuel Beckett

Texts which 'borrow' characters:
Jean Rhys in *Wide Sargasso Sea* (Penguin, 1981) borrows from Charlotte Brontë's *Jane Eyre* (Chatto and Windus, 1946)
Sue Roe in *Estella: her expectations* (Harvester Wheatsheaf, 1983) borrows from Charles Dickens' *Great Expectations* (Oxford University Press)
Tom Stoppard in *Rosencrantz and Guildenstern Are Dead* (Faber and Faber, 1968) borrows from Shakespeare's *Hamlet* (Methuen, 1982)

Novels which use historical characters or events:
G., John Berger (Hogarth Press, 1989)
The Passion, Jeanette Winterson (Bloomsbury Publishing, 1987)
Midnight's Children, Salman Rushdie (Jonathan Cape, 1981)

Parodies:
The Faber Book of Parodies (ed.) Simon Brett (Faber and Faber, 1984)
Wendy Cope's collection of verse, *Making Cocoa for Kingsley Amis* (Faber and Faber, 1986) has some good parodies of modern poets.

POPULAR FICTION

GENRE

It was 5 o'clock on Thursday afternoon when Peter opened the door of the train...

- *This is the opening sentence of your novel. Choose two of the following types of fiction and continue the narrative in the appropriate manner. For each 'style' write the first page and give it a suitable title:*
  - *a) a romance;*
  - *b) a spy story;*
  - *c) a science fiction story;*
  - *d) a thriller;*
  - *e) a best-selling biography of a film or pop star.*
- *Try your novel openings out on other readers. How convinced were they by your style?*
  What particular features did you use to define each genre?

We often recognise a certain formula in a text; there may be features of narrative, language or structure that it has in common with other texts. Popular forms of fiction are often seen as formulaic and easily identified by the way they are published and read. It might, for example, be sold as one of a series with distinctive covers, or through magazines aimed at readers with a particular interest or mail-order bookclubs.

- *Read through the following extracts and identify features which place them in a particular genre:*

1 They were assembled in the lounge—Marshall, the Redferns, Rosamund Darnley and Hercule Poirot.

They sat there silent—waiting. . . .

The door opened and Dr. Neasdon came in. He said curtly:

'I've done all I can. She may pull through—but I'm bound to tell you that there's not much hope.'

He paused. Marshall, his face stiff, his eyes a cold frosty blue asked:

'How did she get hold of the stuff?'

Neasdon opened the door again and beckoned.

The chambermaid came into the room. She had been crying:

Neasdon said:

'Just tell us again what you saw?'

2   The women in the room are whispering, almost talking, so great is their excitement.

'Who is it?' I hear behind me.

'Ofwayne. No. Ofwarren.'

'Show-off,' a voice hisses, and this is true. A woman that pregnant doesn't have to go out, doesn't have to go shopping. The daily walk is no longer prescribed, to keep her abdominal muscles in working order. She needs only the floor exercises, the breathing drill. She could stay at her house. And it's dangerous for her to be out, there must be a Guardian standing outside the door, waiting for her. Now that she's the carrier of life, she is closer to death, and needs special security. Jealousy could get her, it's happened before. All children are wanted now, but not by everyone.

3   'No – no – Jane; you must not go. No – I have touched you, heard you, felt the comfort of your presence – the sweetness of your consolation: I cannot give up these joys. I have little left in myself – I must have you. The world may laugh – may call me absurd, selfish – but it does not signify. My very soul demands you: it will be satisfied: or it will take deadly vengeance on its frame.'

4   Meanwhile she worked, she raised her son Sanxi, and she waited. She may have been helped through her solitude by her four sisters-in-law and by the wise woman who had counselled her during her bewitchment ... But she surely reflected on her life, dividing it into thirds as she did later when presenting herself to the judge at Rieux: the nine or ten years of her marriage, the years of her waiting, which lengthened into eight or more. Beyond a young womanhood with only a brief period of sexuality, beyond a marriage in which her husband understood her little, may have feared her, and surely abandoned her, Bertrande dreamed of a husband and lover who would come back and be different. Then in the summer of 1556, a man presented himself to her as the long-lost Martin Guerre.

• *For each extract explain how you arrived at an identification, and discuss the difficulties you encountered in doing so. (The origins of these extracts are given at the end of the chapter.)*

One of the difficulties of 'placing' fiction in this way is that categories are always shifting: popular fiction is much influenced by social change (for example hospital romances are now more common than governess romances) and writers attempt to blur labels by putting a new perspective on a familiar form. Why might a writer wish to combine science fiction and feminism, for example? Would it be possible to combine romance with pornography?

POPULAR FICTION FOR BOYS AND GIRLS

Looking at the forms of 'popular fiction' does not take us very far in understanding its popularity, nor reveal the way it is related to the culture we live in. We need to ask questions about how the book is marketed and read, and how the patterns of characterisation and narrative relate to readers' perceptions of themselves and to other popular images in society.

Obviously men and women read fiction of all types but if we ask what types of popular fiction appeal particularly to males then we might produce a list that includes intrigue and adventure, spy stories, thrillers, detective novels or stories concerning predominantly male worlds, such as war or westerns. For women, on the other hand, there seems to be one primary category: romance. Romance is considered almost exclusively a female interest, though it is not unlikely that women also read thrillers and science fiction, for example.

In fact romance outsells most other areas of fiction. It is one of the few highly profitable areas of publishing. Such a large number of women read romance (it is suggested that at any given moment 50% of women reading are reading romance) that the popular image of the bored housewife reading to escape can hardly be an adequate explanation of the readership or the appeal of the books.

- *Discuss your own experiences of romantic fiction, not only in novels, but also in magazines or on television.*
- *Where does their appeal or lack of interest lie for you?*
- *Is your reaction to romantic fiction affected by your gender, your education or reading habits? In what ways?*

A Mills and Boon novel is sold in rather a different way from other fiction. It is often bought in newsagents, corner shops and bookstalls, or circulated through mailing lists, friendship groups and jumble sales. We think of buying a 'Mills and Boon' rather than a work by a particular author as we might do with more highly regarded fiction.

- *Here is the promotion page from one Mills and Boon novel encouraging the reader to buy more. Predict the storyline of each one:*

SCORPIO SUMMER
Frances had done old Lady Ravenscar a very good turn, as a result of which

the two had become friends – and the old lady was particularly anxious that Frances should meet her son Felix. Someone ought to have warned Frances that the gentleman in question was a Scorpio, the sign whose sting can sometimes be fatal. Or would she be able, once she had met him, to work that one out of herself?

EVERY WISE MAN

When Olivia Darcy went to work as secretary in the delightful Raynor household, she got on happily with everybody – with her boss, Charles Raynor, and two of his sons, Paul and Julian. Everybody except one, the third son, Matthew, who had seemed to take an instant dislike to her. But why? It wasn't as if he could possibly know her secret . . .

DEAR VILLAIN

Liz was looking forward immensely to her new job as deputy stage manager at the splendid new Queensbridge Civic Theatre – until she learned that the director was going to be Adam Carlyon. For Adam Carlyon was a man she had no wish whatsoever to meet again . . .

COUNTRY COUSIN

A hard-up parson's daughter from Yorkshire, Eleanor might have felt out of her depth when she came south to stay with her mother's friends, the well-off Mansel family. But they couldn't have been nicer or kinder, and Eleanor liked them immensely. What a pity she couldn't feel the same way about the son of the family, the uncompromising Edward . . .

- *Discuss your predictions.*
- *What are the common features of such narratives?*
- *What satisfactions do you think they offer the reader?*

THE APPEAL OF POPULAR FICTION

The popularity of 'popular fiction' is difficult to explain for the literary critic. How is it that literature dismissed as shallow 'pulp' is so successful? It is impossible to believe that innocent readers have been duped by advertising on so many occasions, or that they are too stupid to put aside a worthless read. The fact is that people carry on buying popular fiction because it satisfies them in some way, even if it is not a way approved by the literary critic.

So what is the appeal of popular fiction for its readers? One answer may lie in the underlying themes and scenarios of popular fiction, which touch on our immediate concerns. We may not be little lost orphans, but we know what it is to crave love. Popular fiction appeals to commonplace feelings and provides a playground for the imagination: a place where everyday hopes and anxieties can be played through.

From the earliest age, literature offers a safe context for the play of imagination. Many of the myths we learn in childhood retain their

fascination for adults. The *Superman* fiction is an interesting example. Saved from destruction on his home planet, Krypton, Superman acquires super-powers as he arrives on Earth. Brought up in a typical American town, he shelters behind the secret identity of bumbling Clark Kent, a likeable but inept character whom no one would suspect of being a super-hero. Fortunately, Superman is a benevolent type, fond of the American way of life, using his amazing powers of flight, strength and near-invulnerability to protect innocent people, especially from crime. His ability to peel off his beleaguered everyday identity and turn into a 'man of steel' is a deeply appealing fantasy which may be shared by many readers. The Superman fiction appeals to deep desires.

- *What parallels can you see between Superman and another character from popular fiction, James Bond (see page 123)?*
- *Discuss the following familiar scenarios from popular fiction and consider where their appeal may lie for the reader. Can you identify ways in which they address everyday concerns?*
  - *a) metamorphosis (changing into other states or personalities) in horror fiction. eg. vampires and werewolves;*
  - *b) journeying on a quest or mission, overcoming challenges on the way;*
  - *c) working in a secret service, unravelling complex information from a web of intrigue.*

POPULAR FICTION AND LITERARY QUALITY

The distinction between 'popular' fiction and 'quality' fiction is sometimes hard to draw. Critics commonly pay attention to the depth of characterisation, the originality of the plot and the sophistication of the style. Even then, it is hard to see why some qualities are considered more worthy than others.

One of the extracts below is taken from the Mills and Boon novel, *Country Cousin*, described earlier in this section. The other is from the 'classic' Jane Austen novel, *Pride and Prejudice*. Before you read the pieces, consider the attitudes you bring with you to these types of fiction – what differences do you expect to find between the two extracts?

1   Edward was an irregular visitor, coming and going without warning, and she had not seen him since that first day. He had a flat in town and working hours were spent between the family business and the antique shop, in which his mother and sister also had an interest. What he did outside business hours was anyone's guess, and his private life was kept strictly private, although glossy photographs in society magazines showed him escorting some beautiful girl or another, indicating that he was no hermit. First impressions, although often not true ones, had a habit of sticking, and Eleanor's were not favourable. The fact that he made her feel extremely young and gauche did not help, and despite the lazy manner, she felt there

was an underlying ruthlessness in him. She had every intention of keeping out of his way, for he brought out the worst in her, but some pricking of the thumbs told her that when Edward was around he would make his presence felt. She acknowledged that his looks were striking, but inscrutable faces always made her uneasy, she preferred a more open, friendlier disposition, and men whose eyebrows met – and his were extraordinarily dark and thick – she was mistrustful of. She guessed his was a popular name on the county guest lists – thirty and unmarried, presentable and wealthy, he was a challenge to every mother with a marriageable daughter, and Eleanor considered that many an eye would gleam with untold satisfaction when Edward Mansel put his foot across the threshold!

2 Mr Bingley was good looking and gentlemanlike; he had a pleasant countenance, and easy, unaffected manners. His sisters were fine women, with an air of decided fashion. His brother-in-law, Mr Hurst, merely looked the gentleman; but his friend Mr Darcy soon drew the attention of the room by his fine, tall person, handsome features, noble mien; and the report which was in general circulation within five minutes after his entrance, of his having ten thousand a year. The gentlemen pronounced him to be a fine figure of a man, the ladies declared he was much handsomer than Mr Bingley, and he was looked at with great admiration for about half the evening, till his manners gave a disgust which turned the tide of his popularity; for he was discovered to be proud, to be above his company, and above being pleased; and not all his large estate in Derbyshire could then save him from having a most forbidding, disagreeable countenance, and being unworthy to be compared with his friend.

- *How far were your expectations of differences between the two texts confirmed?*
- *Do the passages seem related in any way?*
- *Is it possible to argue that there is a difference in quality between the two extracts?*

HAPPY ENDINGS

What expectations do you have of the endings of fiction? This is an important question because the conclusion of a novel is a way of passing judgement on characters, particularly in the case of the traditional happy ending which rewards the 'good' characters with marriage, wealth and success.

- *Read this complete short story by Margaret Atwood:*

HAPPY ENDINGS

John and Mary meet. What happens next? If you want a happy ending, try A.

A. John and Mary fall in love and get married. They both have worthwhile and remunerative jobs which they find stimulating and challenging. They buy a charming house. Real estate values go up. Eventually, when they can afford live-in help, they have two children, to whom they are devoted. The children turn out well. John and Mary have a stimulating and challenging sex life and worthwhile friends. They go on fun vacations together. They retire. They both have hobbies which they find stimulating and challenging. Eventually they die. This is the end of the story.

B. Mary falls in love with John but John doesn't fall in love with Mary. He merely uses her body for selfish pleasure and ego gratification of a tepid kind. He comes to her apartment twice a week and she cooks him dinner, you'll notice that he doesn't even consider her worth the price of a dinner out, and after he's eaten the dinner he fucks her and after that he falls asleep, while she does the dishes so he won't think she's untidy, having all those dirty dishes lying around, and puts on fresh lipstick so she'll look good when he wakes up, but when he wakes up he doesn't even notice, he puts on his socks and his shorts and his pants and his shirt and his tie and his shoes, the reverse order from the one in which he took them off. He doesn't take off Mary's clothes, she takes them off herself, she acts as if she's dying for it every time, not because she likes sex exactly, she doesn't, but she wants John to think she does because if they do it often enough surely he'll get used to her, he'll come to depend on her and they will get married, but John goes out the door with hardly so much as a goodnight and three days later he turns up at six o'clock and they do the whole thing over again.

Mary gets run down. Crying is bad for your face, everyone knows that and so does Mary but she can't stop. People at work notice. Her friends tell her John is a rat, a pig, a dog, he isn't good enough for her, but she can't believe it. Inside John, she thinks, is another John, who is much nicer. This other John will emerge like a butterfly from a cocoon, a Jack from a box, a pit from a prune, if the first John is only squeezed enough.

One evening John complains about the food. He has never complained about the food before. Mary is hurt.

Her friends tell her they've seen him in a restaurant with another woman, whose name is Madge. It's not even Madge that finally gets to Mary: it's the restaurant. John has never taken Mary to a restaurant. Mary collects all the sleeping pills and aspirins she can find, and takes them and half a bottle of sherry. You can see what kind of a woman she is by the fact that it's not even whiskey. She leaves a note for John. She hopes he'll discover her and get her to the hospital in time and repent and then they can get married, but this fails to happen and she dies.

John marries Madge and everything continues as in A.

C. John, who is an older man, falls in love with Mary, and Mary, who is only twenty-two, feels sorry for him because he's worried about his hair falling out. She sleeps with him even though she's not in love with him. She met him at work. She's in love with someone called James, who is twenty-two also and not yet ready to settle down.

John on the contrary settled down long ago: this is what is bothering him. John has a steady respectable job and is getting ahead in his field, but Mary isn't impressed by him, she's impressed by James, who has a motorcycle and a fabulous record collection. But James is often away on his motorcycle, being free. Freedom isn't the same for girls, so in the meantime Mary spends Thursday evenings with John. Thursdays are the only days John can get away.

John is married to a woman called Madge and they have two children, a charming house which they bought just before the real estate values went up, and hobbies which they find stimulating and challenging, when they have the time. John tells Mary how important she is to him, but of course he can't leave his wife because a commitment is a commitment. He goes on about this more than is necessary and Mary finds it boring, but older men can keep it up longer so on the whole she has a fairly good time.

One day James breezes in on his motorcycle with some top grade California hybrid and James and Mary get higher than you'd believe possible and they climb into bed. Everything becomes very underwater, but along comes John, who has a key to Mary's apartment. He finds them stoned and entwined. He's hardly in any position to be jealous, considering Madge, but nevertheless he's overcome with despair. Finally he's middle-aged, in two years he'll be bald as an egg and he can't stand it. He purchases a handgun, saying he needs it for target practice – this is the thin part of the plot, but it can be dealt with later – and shoots the two of them and himself.

Madge, after a suitable period of mourning, marries an understanding man called Fred and everything continues as in A, but under different names.

D. Fred and Madge have no problems. They get along exceptionally well and are good at working out any little difficulties that may arise. But their charming house is by the seashore and one day a giant tidal wave approaches. Real estate values go down. The rest of the story is about what caused the tidal wave and how they escape from it. They do, though thousands drown. Some of the story is about how the thousands drown, but Fred and Madge are virtuous and lucky. Finally on high ground they clasp each other, wet and dripping and grateful, and continue as in A.

E. Yes, but Fred has a bad heart. The rest of the story is about how kind and understanding they both are until Fred dies. Then Madge devotes herself to charity work until the end of A. If you like, it can be 'Madge', 'cancer', 'guilty and confused', and 'bird watching'.

F. If you think this is all too bourgeois, make John a revolutionary and Mary a counterespionage agent and see how far that gets you. Remember, this is Canada. You'll still end up with A, though in between you may get a lustful brawling saga of passionate involvement, a chronicle of our times, sort of.

You'll have to face it, the endings are the same however you slice it. Don't be deluded by any other endings, they're all fake, either deliberately fake, with malicious intent to deceive, or just motivated by excessive optimism if not by downright sentimentality.

The only authentic ending is the one provided here:
John and Mary die. John and Mary die. John and Mary die.

So much for endings. Beginnings are always more fun. True connoisseurs, however, are known to favour the stretch in between, since it's the hardest to do anything with.

That's about all that can be said for plots, which anyway are just one thing after another, a what and a what and a what.

Now try How and Why.

- *What types of fiction are ridiculed here?*
- *What criticism does the story make of conventional endings?*
- *What ideas does this story offer about the nature of fiction in general?*

Reading List

For texts trying to break into genres, you could try feminist science fiction or feminist detective fiction. There is a series produced by The Women's Press and novels such as Marge Piercy's *Woman on The Edge of Time* (The Women's Press, 1978), Angela Carter's *The Passion of New Eve* (Virago, 1982), Dr Hoffman's *The Infernal Desire Machines* (Penguin, 1982) or Margaret Atwood's *The Handmaid's Tale* (Jonathan Cape, 1986).

Texts mentioned in the chapter include *The Return of Martin Guerre* by Natalie Zemon Davies (Penguin, 1985) which raises the problems of fiction derived from historical reconstruction.

For a feminist look at aspects of popular culture try the essays in Rosalind Coward's *Female Desire* (Granada, 1984).

Extracts used in the 'Genre' section

1   is from *Evil Under the Sun* by Agatha Christie.
2   is an extract from Margaret Atwood's *The Handmaid's Tale*, a novel with feminist interest set in the future.
3   is from Charlotte Brontë's *Jane Eyre*.
4   is from *The Return of Martin Guerre*, by Natalie Zemon Davies, which reconstructs from historical documents the story of a French medieval peasant who completely assumes another man's identity and life.

MAKING SENSE

HE ROLE OF THE READER

THE ACT OF READING

- *What happens when you read? How does your mind go about making sense of the story or poem before it? Try recording the mental process of reading by making notes on an empty sheet by your side as you read. Write down any thoughts, questions, images, ideas or comments which pass through your mind as you read the following poem, and then allow yourself about five minutes to re-read it and develop your response:*

UNDER A RAMSHACKLE RAINBOW

A dead tree.
On a rotten branch sit two wingless birds. Among leaves
on the ground a man is searching for his hands.
It is fall.

A stagnant marsh.
On a mossy stone sits the man angling. The hook
is stuck in the waterlily.
The waterlily is stuck in the mud.

An overgrown ruin.
In the grass the man sleeps sitting up. A raindrop descends
in slow-motion through space.
Somewhere in the grass a pike flounders.

A dry well.
At the bottom lies a dead fly. In the wood nearby
a spider gropes through the fog.
The man is trapped in the spiderweb on the horizon.

An abandoned ant hill.
Above a little woodmarsh floats the man. The sun

is just going down. The man has already stopped growing.
The ants gather on the shore.

Ingemar Gustafson,
translated from the Swedish by May Swenson

- *Compare your reactions with those of other people in a small group and look also at the variety of responses recorded on pages 140 and 141 by students doing the same exercise.*

- *Try the exercise again with this short story:*

AN EVERYDAY OCCURRENCE

An everyday occurrence: the enduring of it a matter of everyday heroism. A has an important deal to conclude with B from the neighbouring village of H. He goes to H for the preliminary discussion, gets there and back in ten minutes each way, and at home boasts of this unusual rapidity. The next day he goes to H again, this time for the final settlement of the deal; since this is likely to take several hours, A sets out early in the morning; but although all the attendant circumstances, at least in A's opinion, are exactly the same as on the previous day, this time it takes him ten hours to get to H. When he arrives there weary in the evening, he is told that B, annoyed at A's failure to arrive, has gone across to A's village half an hour ago, they ought to have met each other on the way. A is advised to wait, B is sure to be back soon. But A, anxious about the deal, at once sets out again and hurries home. This time without particularly noticing the fact, he covers the distance in no more than an instant. At home he is informed that B had actually arrived there early in the day, even before A's departure, indeed that he had met A on the doorstep and reminded him about the deal, but A had said he had no time just then, he had to go off at once on a matter of urgency. In spite of this incomprehensible behaviour on A's part, however, B had nevertheless remained here to wait for A. It was true that he had already inquired many times whether A was not back yet, but he was still upstairs in A's room. Happy at still being able to see B now and explain everything to him, A runs upstairs. He is almost at the top when he stumbles, strains a tendon, and, almost fainting with pain, incapable even of crying out, just whimpering there in the dark, he sees and hears how B – he is not sure whether a great distance off or just close to him – stamps down the stairs in a fury and disappears for good.

Franz Kafka

- *What are the skills involved in 'reading' other media such as paintings, television, talk and theatrical performances? Try the same exercise as before with the drawing by Rauch opposite, jotting down your responses as they unfold.*

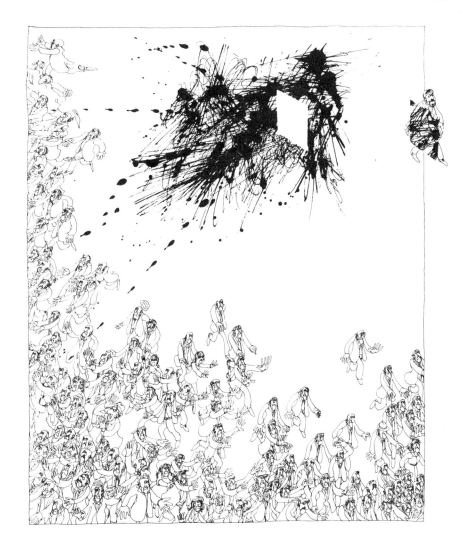

- *In what ways is the experience of reading a picture the same as or different from reading written literature?*
- *In small groups, discuss the various mental activities which occurred and the strategies you employed to make sense of the three items above.*

Readers are not sponges, passively absorbing the text. They re-create the text according to their own knowledge and experience, within the framework provided by the author. This re-creation may prompt many kinds of mental activity: sudden images which flash through the mind; questions and exclamations about aspects of the text; acts of anticipation, guesswork and re-evaluation as the reader goes deeper into the text, and the relish of re-reading the best moments.

But readers are not completely free to create the text in their own way: they are directed by the writer through the language. The writer guides the responses of the readers but allows room for the individual to imagine it in their own way. The following exercise demonstrates the presence of the writer's guiding hand but also the diversity of individual responses. The extract is a complete section from a Margaret Atwood piece entitled 'Significant Moments in the Life of My Mother', but you are asked to read it in stages, and to discuss after each extract what mental images you see in your mind's eye, what your chief reaction is and how your feelings change as the piece unfolds.

● *Read and discuss each extract before moving on to the next bit:*

> When my mother was very small, someone gave her a basket of baby chicks for Easter.

and now this:

> When my mother was very small, someone gave her a basket of baby chicks for Easter. They all died.

and now this:

> When my mother was very small, someone gave her a basket of baby chicks for Easter. They all died.
> 'I didn't know you weren't supposed to pick them up,' says my mother.

and now this:

> When my mother was very small, someone gave her a basket of baby chicks for Easter. They all died.
> I didn't know you weren't supposed to pick them up,' says my mother. 'Poor little things. I laid them out in a row on a board, with their little legs sticking out straight as pokers, and wept over them. I'd loved them to death.'

and now this:

> When my mother was very small, someone gave her a basket of baby chicks for Easter. They all died.
> 'I didn't know you weren't supposed to pick them up,' says my mother. 'Poor little things. I laid them out in a row on a board, with their little legs sticking out straight as pokers, and wept over them. I'd loved them to death.'
> Possibly this story is meant by my mother to illustrate her own stupidity, and also her sentimentality. We are to understand she wouldn't do such a thing now.

and finally:

> When my mother was very small, someone gave her a basket of baby chicks for Easter. They all died.
> 'I didn't know you weren't supposed to pick them up,' says my mother.

'Poor little things. I laid them out in a row on a board, with their little legs sticking out straight as pokers, and wept over them. I'd loved them to death.'

Possibly this story is meant by my mother to illustrate her own stupidity, and also her sentimentality. We are to understand she wouldn't do such a thing now.

Possibly it's a commentary on the nature of love; though, knowing my mother, this is unlikely.

- *Compare responses, noting the similarities and the differences of individual responses.*
- *Can you account for the similarities and differences? In what way has the writer guided her readers to have a similar response? Give examples of differences in your readings. Notice how different people see different images and have different reactions. How do you account for these differences?*

Texts are played through in the individual imaginations of their readers. Your experience of *Wuthering Heights* may not be the one enjoyed by your neighbour.

PLACING THE READER

Writers invite us to share their visions through the words they choose. Quite literally, this may mean that we see events from the same standpoint as the narrator. Read these two passages and notice where it places you as an onlooker:

1 He was struggling in every direction, he was the centre of the writhing and kicking knot of his own body. There was no up or down, no light and no air. He felt his mouth open of itself and the shrieked word burst out,

'Help!'

When the air had gone with the shriek, water came in to fill its place – burning water, hard in the throat and mouth as stones that hurt. He hutched his body towards the place where air had been but now it was gone and there was nothing but black, choking welter. His body let loose its panic and his mouth strained open till the hinges of his jaw hurt. Water thrust in, down, without mercy. Air came with it for a moment so that he fought in what might have been the right direction. But water reclaimed him and spun so that knowledge of where the air might be was erased completely. Turbines were screaming in his ears and green sparks flew out from the centre like tracer. There was a piston engine too, racing out of gear and making the whole universe shake. Then for a moment there was air like a cold mask against his face and he bit into it. Air and water mixed, dragged down into his body like gravel. Muscles, nerves and blood, struggling lungs, a machine in the head, they worked for one moment in an ancient pattern. The lumps of hard water jerked in the gullet, the lips came together and parted, the tongue arched, the brain lit a neon track.

'Moth—'

(from *Pincher Martin* by William Golding)

2   Nothing can describe the confusion of thought which I felt when I sunk into the water; for tho' I swam very well, yet I could not deliver my self from the waves so as to draw breath, till that wave having driven me, or rather carried me a vast way on towards the shore, and having spent it self, went back, and left me upon the land almost dry, but half dead with the water I took in. I had so much presence of mind as well as breath left, that seeing my self nearer the main land than I expected, I got upon my feet, and endeavoured to make on towards the land as fast as I could, before another wave should return, and take me up again. But I soon found it was impossible to avoid it; for I saw the sea come after me as high as a great hill, and as furious as an enemy which I had no means or strength to contend with; my business was to hold my breath, and raise myself upon the water, if I could; and so by swimming to preserve my breathing, and pilot my self towards the shore, if possible, my greatest concern now being, that the sea, as it would carry me a great way towards the shore when it came on, might not carry me back again with it when it gave back towards the sea.

The wave that came upon me again, buried me at once 20 or 30 foot deep in its own body; and I could feel my self carried with a mighty force and swiftness towards the shore a very great way; but I held my breath, and assisted my self to swim still forward with all my might.

(from *Robinson Crusoe* by Daniel Defoe)

- *Compare your reactions to the two drowning men. What sense of involvement did you experience in each case?*
- *What is your 'viewpoint' in each case?*
- *What aspects of the writing have placed you there? You may find it useful to consider:*
  a) *who tells or controls the narrative;*
  b) *the nature of the experiences described;*
  c) *the sentence structure; who/what is doing the doing;*
  d) *the pace, structure and logic of the passages;*
  e) *the use of imagery.*

You will realise that the narrator – the voice telling the story – has placed you at a certain distance from the events in each passage. This is a deliberate choice by the writers. In many ways, these two passages illustrate two views of mankind: Defoe's first person narrator is typical of his time, full of confidence, control and initiative, whereas Golding's twentieth century man is presented as a victim, powerless, in a hostile and incomprehensible universe.

NARRATORS AND IMPLIED READERS

Besides literally placing the reader so that we share perspectives with the narrator, language also has the effect of placing us in a particular relationship with the author. Where some narrators address their readers directly, even conducting leisurely informal chats with them, others do not seem to acknowledge their existence and the story seems to be told by an all-seeing presence. Between these two extremes are a range of different narrative approaches.

- *To illustrate this point, prepare a reading of the following pieces to be read aloud to an audience. Notice in particular:*
- about the narrator: *Who seems to be speaking? What is their manner? Describe the kind of person you imagine them to be;*
- about the person addressed: *Who is addressed? What assumptions does the voice or narrator make about the reader and the relationship between them?;*
- about writers and readers: *Are the writer and the narrator one and the same? How can you know? Is the implied reader the same as the actual reader – and can you really speak for anyone other than yourself?*

I   MORTAL COMBAT

It is because you were my friend,
    I fought you as the devil fights.
Whatever fortune God may send,
    For once I set the world to rights.

And that was when I thrust you down,
    And stabbed you twice and twice again,
Because you dared take off your crown,
    And be a man like other men.

Mary Coleridge

2 Once upon a time there was an old pig called Aunt Pettitoes. She had eight of a family: four little girl pigs, called Cross-patch, Suck-suck, Yock-yock and Spot; and four little boy pigs, called Alexander, Pigling Bland, Chin-chin and Stumpy. Stumpy had had an accident to his tail.

The eight little pigs had very fine appetites. 'Yus, yus, yus! they eat and indeed they *do* eat!' said Aunt Pettitoes, looking at her family with pride. Suddenly there were fearful squeals; Alexander had squeezed inside the hoops of the pig trough and stuck.

Aunt Pettitoes and I dragged him out by the hind legs.

Chin-chin was already in disgrace; it was washing day, and he had eaten a piece of soap. And presently in a basket of clean clothes, we found another dirty little pig. 'Tchut, tut, tut! whichever is this?' grunted Aunt Pettitoes. Now all the pig family are pink, or pink with black spots, but this pig child was smutty black all over; when it had been popped into a tub, it proved to be Yock-yock.

I went into the garden; there I found Cross-patch and Suck-suck rooting up carrots. I whipped them myself and led them out by the ears. Cross-patch tried to bite me.

'Aunt Pettitoes, Aunt Pettitoes! you are a worthy person, but your family is not well brought up. Every one of them has been in mischief except Spot and Pigling Bland.'

'Yus, yus!' sighed Aunt Pettitoes. 'And they drink bucketfuls of milk; I shall have to get another cow! Good little Spot shall stay at home to do the house-work; but the others must go. Four little boy pigs and four little girl pigs are too many altogether.' 'Yus, yus, yus,' said Aunt Pettitoes, 'there will be more to eat without them.'

(from The Tale of Pigling Bland by Beatrix Potter)

3 If Miss Rebecca Sharp had determined in her heart upon making the conquest of this big beau, I don't think, ladies, we have any right to blame her; for though the task of husband-hunting is generally, and with becoming modesty, intrusted by young persons to their mammas, recollect that Miss Sharp had no kind parent to arrange these delicate matters for her, and that if she did not get a husband for herself, there was no one else in the wide world who would take the trouble off her hands. What causes young people to 'come *out*', but the noble ambition of matrimony? What sends them trooping to watering-places? What keeps them dancing till five o'clock in the morning through a whole mortal season? What causes them to labour at pianoforte sonatas, and to learn four songs from a fashionable master at a guinea a lesson, and to play the harp if they have handsome arms and neat elbows, and to wear Lincoln green toxophilite hats and feathers, but that they may bring down some 'desirable' young man with those killing bows and arrows of theirs? What causes respectable parents to take up their carpets, set their houses topsy-turvy, and spend a fifth of their year's income in ball suppers and iced champagne? Is it sheer love of their species, and an unadulterated wish to see young people happy and dancing? Psha! they want to marry their daughters; and, as honest Mrs Sedley has, in the depths of her kind heart, already arranged a score of little schemes for the settlement of her Amelia, so also had our beloved but unprotected Rebecca determined to do her very best to secure the husband, who was even more necessary for her than for her friend. She had a vivid imagination; she had, besides, read the *Arabian Nights* and *Guthrie's Geography*; and it is a fact, that while she was dressing for dinner, and after she had asked Amelia whether her brother was very rich, she had built for herself a most magnificent castle in the air.

(from Vanity Fair by William Makepeace Thackeray)

4 'Shall I tell you?'
   'What?'
   'Shall I?'
   'Tell me what?' said Jan.
   Jan picked up a fistful of earth and trickled it down the neck of his shirt.
   'Hey!'
   'Stop fooling, then.'
   Tom shook his trouser legs. 'That's rotten. I'm all gritty.'
   Jan hung her arms over the motorway fence. Cars went by like brush marks. 'Where are they going? They look so serious.'
   'Well,' said Tom. 'Let's work it out. That one there is travelling south at, say, one hundred and twenty kilometres per hour, on a continental shelf drifting east at about five centimetres per year –'
   'I might've guessed –'
   '– on a planet rotating at about nine hundred and ninety kilometres per

hour at this degree of latitude, at a mean orbital velocity of thirty kilometres per second –'

'Really?'

'– in a solar system travelling at a mean galactic velocity of two hundred and twenty kilometres per second, in a galaxy that probably has a random motion –'

'Knickers.'

'– random knickers of about one hundred kilometres per second, in a universe that appears to be expanding at about one hundred and sixteen kilometres per second per megaparsec.'

Jan scooped up more earth.

'The short answer's Birmingham,' he said, and ducked.

(from *Red Shift* by Alan Garner)

In accepting the perspective of the author, the reader also accepts a package deal of attitudes and values. This aspect of reading is explored further in the chapter 'The Voice of Reason'.

Reading List

The Cool Web edited by Meek, Warlow and Barton (The Bodley Head, 1978) is a collection of essays about reading and writing children's books.

The Rhetoric of Fiction by Wayne Booth (University of Chicago Press, 1961) is a classic study about narrators and the art of narrative.

The Craft of Fiction by Percy Lubbock (Jonathan Cape, 1921) talks about the novelist's art.

Ways of Seeing by John Berger (BBC/Penguin, 1972) gives a stimulating introduction to the problems of interpretation. It is vividly presented and includes three 'essays' in picture form.

Letters to Alice by Fay Weldon (Hodder and Stoughton, 1985) is a series of fictitious letters about reading the novels of Jane Austen. It provides an interesting alternative format for reflective criticism.

Responses to 'Under a Ramshackle Rainbow' in 'The Act of Reading'

I   Wendy

Old, rotten, depression, ~~searching~~ searching, American.
Smells, all things depend on something or lead to
something, not one is to blame.
Overtaken, 'sleeping beauty' laziness.
Underwater feeling — everything moves slowly.
In - security, clostraphobic, no escape.
No life, people left
Unusual 'the' man, gives him importance
Personality.
End, (but hope the ants are still together)
↓ but 'just', so maybe more hope.

2   GEOFF

3   SARA

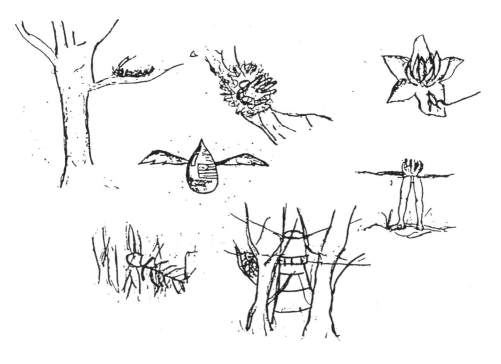

4 CLAIRE

Very odd. Slightly sadistic (a man searching for his hands)
Old and overgrown images. Slight storybookish : wingless
birds. I keep trying to include a rainbow. Things
that ~~came~~ cannot happen.

    Lots of blank statements. Each stanza begins with
an odd, perhaps impossible, certainly not pleasant, image.
The stanza then goes on to include something else
odd about the first image.

    Seems to be a ~~one~~ more adult, more frightening
child's story. Making ~~s~~ a story or fairy tale and
making some of the images more realistic + frightening.
The title gives us the idea that it is an odd fairy tale.

THE MEDIATION OF MEANING

TRANSLATIONS

The language we use is permeated with all the values, assumptions and beliefs we hold. It is too simple to see words as empty containers into which we pour our meanings. This point is particularly clear when we compare two versions of the same event: no two interpretations are the same. Even our own memories of experience change as we grow older. We see things differently, and our language changes to reflect this.

Translations offer telling examples of the way two people may construe the same text differently. In looking at the following example, it is important to recognise that both these translators are experts in their fields: we cannot dismiss differences simply in terms of 'bad' translation. But we can say that translating from one language to another is no simple matter. The syntax, vocabulary and atmosphere of an original work can never be exactly reproduced in another language.

The following extracts are from a short story called *A Lady with a Dog* by Anton Chekov. There are two translations from the Russian – the first by Ronald Hingley, a native English speaker and the second by David Magarshak, a native Russian speaker. Compare the two extracts paying particular attention to the italicised expressions.

1 'If she has no husband or friends here *she might be worth picking up*,' *calculated* Gurov.

He was still in his thirties but had a twelve-year-old daughter and two schoolboy sons. *His marriage had been arranged early* – during his second college year – and now his wife seemed half as old again as he. She was a tall, dark-browed woman: *outspoken*, *earnest*, *stolid* and – she maintained – an 'intellectual'. She was a great reader, she favoured spelling reform, she called her husband 'Demetrius' instead of plain 'Dmitry', while he privately thought her narrow-minded, inelegant and slow on the uptake. He was afraid of her, and disliked being at home. *He had begun deceiving her long ago, and his infidelities were frequent* – which is probably why *he nearly always spoke so disparagingly of women, calling them an 'inferior species' when the subject cropped up.*

2   'If she's here without her husband and without any friends,' *thought* Gurov, *'it wouldn't be a bad idea to strike up an acquaintance with her.'*

He was not yet forty, but he had a twelve-year-old daughter and two schoolboy sons. *He had been married off* when he was still in his second year at the university, and his wife seemed to him now to be almost twice his age. She was a tall, black-browed woman, *erect, dignified, austere,* and, as she liked to describe herself, a 'thinking person'. She was a great reader, preferred the new 'advanced' spelling, called her husband by the more formal 'Dimitry' and not the familiar 'Dmitry'; and though he secretly considered her not particularly intelligent, narrow-minded, and inelegant, he was afraid of her and disliked being at home. *He had been unfaithful to her for a long time,* he was often unfaithful to her, and that was why, perhaps, he almost *always spoke ill of women, and when men discussed women in his presence, he described them as the lower breed.*

- *What differences in emphasis do you detect between the italicised expressions?*
- *How do these differences in translation influence our overall reactions towards the passage and the people in it?*

Simply, there can be no completely successful translations, because the original remains the ultimate best version of itself. Take Chaucer's *Canterbury Tales* for example, which has been 'translated' as though from a foreign language by generations of school students for their examiners, though the original language is still accessible to modern speakers. This extract is part of the immensely entertaining speech of the Wife of Bath as she reflects upon her various adventures in married life:

> But, Lord Crist! when that it remembereth me
> Upon my yowthe, and on my jolitee,
> It tikleth me aboute myn herte roote.
> Unto this day it dooth myn herte boote
> That I have had my world as in my time.
> But age, allas, that wole envenime,
> Hath me biraft my beautee and my pith.
> Lat go, farewel; the devel go therwith!
> The flour is goon, ther is namoore to telle;
> The bren, as I best kan, now moste I selle . . .

Here is a 'modern prose rendering' of that speech by David Wright written in 1964:

But, Lord Christ! When it all comes back to me, and I recall my youth and gaiety, it tickles me to the roots of my heart. To this day it does my heart good that in my time I've had my fling. But age, alas! that cankers everything, has stripped me of my beauty and go. Goodbye, let them go, and the devil go with them! What's left to say? The flour's gone, and now I must sell the bran as best I may . . .

- *What aspects of Chaucer's original are enhanced, spoiled or lost in translation?*

Now consider this version by Neville Coghill written in 1951:

> But Christ! Whenever it comes back to me,
> When I recall my youth and jollity,
> It fairly warms the cockles of my heart!
> This very day I feel a pleasure start,
> Yes, I can feel it tickling at the root.
> Lord, how it does me good! I've had my fruit,
> I've had my world and time, I've had my fling!
> But age that comes to poison everything
> Has taken all my beauty and my pith.
> Well, let it go, the devil go therewith!
> The flour is gone, there is no more to say,
> And I must sell the bran as best I may . . .

- *What differences of approach do you notice between this version and the Wright one?*
- *Does either of the translations strike you as 'better' than the other, and what is it that recommends it?*
- *What light do these translations throw upon the original work for you?*

The translation of bibles raises particularly important questions because believers direct their lives according to their guidance and in many cases accept them as the authentic word of God. For them, its meanings are sacred and absolute. Most religions have a holy book, but not many people are able to read these texts in the original language. The Christian bible, for example, has been translated from Hebrew into Greek and then into English. In 1961 a distinguished panel of translators was appointed to prepare a modern translation of the bible, and the preface explains how individuals presented drafts to the panel, who

> . . . met together and discussed the draft around a table, verse by verse, sentence by sentence. Each member brought his view about the meaning of the original to the judgement of his fellows, and discussion was continued until they reached a common mind. There is probably no member of the panel who has not found himself compelled to give up, perhaps with lingering regret, a cherished view about the meaning of this or that difficult or doubtful passage.

- *What implications does the process of translation have for people who read the scriptures?*

THE REPRESENTATION OF EXPERIENCE

The past is never there waiting to be discovered, to be recognised for exactly what it is.

John Berger

You cannot just 'write the truth'; you have to write it *for* and *to* somebody, somebody who can do something with it.

Bertolt Brecht

When we record experience, whether far back in the past or recent, whether an international event like a war or a personal one like a domestic row, we are often seeking to describe what *really* happened. But how possible is this?

The following extract is from the transcript of a conversation with a woman who was born in 1901. She had recently attended the 100th anniversary celebration of the Brighton Women's Co-operative Guild, a radical campaigning and social group which sprang out of the Co-operative movement:

... and my mother joined the Central Guild before I was born and she said – oh, she always told us how she did it – because my father, my father when my mother met him, he was in lodgings and the person he was lodging with was one of the early suffragettes who went on hunger strike in prison and all that – and she said to my mother one day, she said, 'I've heard that the Co-op have started a Women's Guild, shall we start?' Er, well it was unusual for women to go out to meetings. They decided they would leave it until half past seven when they were supposed to start and they went up the stairs – 'cause they met in an eating house in Cheapside and they'd creep up the stairs to where the women would be meeting and see what they were like. And a Mrs W—— who was there, the wife of one of the Board of Management, well she always stood out there to see if any new people would come along to give them a greeting! And fifty years ago, when the society celebrated its fiftieth birthday and the eldest or longest member of the Guild was invited to the lunch at the Dome where they had a concert and Clem Atlee was guest of honour and my mother had been a member of Central Guild longer than anyone else – a lot of the others had died off – I said last Sunday at the (100 years) celebrations that I am probably the only one who could remember being pushed there – we used to have carpet chairs, pushchairs – I remembered being pushed right down North Road, where we only had one shop – my mother pushed me all the way back ...

The material shown here is a transcript of the spoken word. Punctuation has been added.

- *In groups or as individuals, re-present this material for the different purposes outlined below, selecting, arranging and expressing it in ways which are appropriate to the task:*
  - *a) as an extract from a novel;*
  - *b) as part of a television script – for example for a drama or documentary (give an indication of both pictures and sound);*
  - *c) as part of a chapter in a history book;*
  - *d) as an extract from the local newspaper report of the fiftieth anniversary celebrations.*
  - *Afterwards . . .*
- *Compare results, noting the variety of interpretation.*
- *Discuss the difficulties you faced in adapting the material for different purposes.*
- *On what basis did you select, arrange and express your material in each case?*

We often approach different media with certain assumptions: for example, that a journalist will be more *objective*, able to look at the situation factually without being involved, than a participant and that an imaginative account will be more *subjective* than, for example, a history book. We also tend to equate objectivity with 'truth'. Yet, as the last exercise suggests, all versions of an event involve active editorial decisions. None of them is more authentic than any other. Even the oral account we started with has already been processed by the very act of putting it into words. All language processes thought; none of it offers us a direct line to the experience.

RECOUNTING HIROSHIMA

Towards the end of the Second World War, on 6 August 1945, the first nuclear weapon was used, dropped by the Americans on the Japanese town of Hiroshima. It was an event of enormous significance for history and for ethics, and there is clearly a very particular demand for description of the experience. At the same time, it is a very difficult subject to approach, loaded as it is with political ideas and historical interpretation, and because of the horrifying and disturbing nature of the effects of the bomb.

The extracts which follow are all concerned with the dropping of the nuclear bomb.

The first is from an account by an American journalist, John Hersey, who visited Hiroshima a year after the explosion. An entire edition of the journal *New Yorker* was devoted to his report: for most people in the West this was their first insight into what happened:

At exactly fifteen minutes past eight in the morning, on 6 August 1945, Japanese time, at the moment when the atomic bomb flashed above Hiroshima, Miss Toshiko Sasaki, a clerk in the personnel department at the

East Asia Tin Works, had just sat down at her place in the plant office and was turning her head to speak to the girl at the next desk. At that same moment, Dr Masakazu Fujii was settling down cross-legged to read the Osaka *Asahi* on the porch of his private hospital, overhanging one of the seven deltaic rivers which divide Hiroshima; Mrs Hatsuyo Nakamura, a tailor's widow, stood by the window of her kitchen watching a neighbour tearing down his house because it lay in the path of an air-raid defence fire lane; Father Wilhelm Kleinsorge, a German priest of the Society of Jesus, reclined in his underwear on a cot on the top floor of his order's three-storey mission house, reading a Jesuit magazine, *Stimmen der Zeit*; Dr Terufumi Sasaki, a young member of the surgical staff of the city's large, modern Red Cross Hospital, walked along one of the hospital corridors with a blood specimen for a Wassermann test in his hand; and the Reverend Mr Kiyoshi Tanimoto, pastor of the Hiroshima Methodist Church, paused at the door of a rich man's house in Koi, the city's western suburb, and prepared to unload a handcart full of things he had evacuated from town in fear of the massive B–29 raid which everyone expected Hiroshima to suffer. A hundred thousand people were killed by the atomic bomb, and these six were among the survivors. They still wonder why they lived when so many others died. Each of them counts many small items of chance or volition – a step taken in time, a decision to go indoors, catching one streetcar instead of the next – that spared him. And now each knows that in the act of survival he lived a dozen lives and saw more death than he ever thought he would see. At the time none of them knew anything.

An aerial photograph of the explosion:

The following are impressions recorded by survivors of Hiroshima:

Rei Ishii age 48 (35)

Yokogawa Bridge above Tenma River, August 6, 1945, 8:30 A.M.
People crying and moaning were running towards the city. I did not know why.
Steam engines were burning at Yokogawa Station.
Tail of cow tied to wire.
Skin of girl's hip was hanging down.
'My baby is dead, isn't she?'

Kinzo Nishida age 82 (654)

The day the A-bomb was dropped

It was about 9:30 A.M., August 6, 1945. While taking my severely wounded wife out to the riverbank by the side of the hill of Nakahiromachi, I was horrified, indeed, at the sight of a stark naked man standing in the rain with his eyeball in his palm. He looked to be in great pain but there was nothing that I could do for him.

I wonder what became of him. Even today, I vividly remember the sight. It was simply miserable.

白島町 縮景園の裏門に通りかゝった
時一人の男の幼児が門にすがって泣いて
いた。声をかけてさわって見ると彼は
死んでいた。吾が子と思えば胸がつまる。

Name unknown (848)

Walking around the back gate of Shukkeien Garden of Hakushima-cho, I saw an infant boy leaning against the gate and heard him crying. When I approached and then touched him, I found that he was dead. To think that he might have been my son made my heart ache.

The following extract is the ending of Maggie Gee's novel *The Burning Book* which takes the form of a conventional family saga. The reader understands right from the start that this engrossing soap opera of family relationships will end in nuclear annihilation, though the political background remains shrouded. The novel uses the experience of Hiroshima throughout, with Japanese 'voices' acting as warnings:

> *Clo-osing time   clo-osing time*
>   *all the endangered   all the endangered*

'You're more wonderful than any machinery,' said Henry hoarsely, putting down his pamphlet, staring at his wife in the sun's red glaze, a lit bright carving of living bronze with her hair spreading out in a metal river and the leaves spreading round her as far as she could see, shivering and rustling in the sunset wind ... how had he, Henry, married such beauty?

It seemed somehow final, this shining Lorna, as if their whole life had led to this moment. 'Do you think we should go?' she said, staring sunwards. He didn't answer, but picked up the curling handful of leaves she had laid on her knees. 'Aren't they lovely Henry? I could stay here for ever ... I'm so happy I could die ... but you're *cold*, my darling. ...'

His teeth were chattering but *he* wasn't cold, his heart beat fiercely in quickening flurries like small birds stirring though there *weren't* any birds, no birds and no people, just the faint voice calling *clo-osing time   time to go home*   but *this* could be home, their home in the garden.

   but in another world long arcs were rising

 (no, it was here   there was only one world despite all those hundreds of leaves of paper   only one world   and one last picture)

 long arcs were falling into the picture, 'We'll never get there,' said Lorna to the moon, and against the red end of the day they saw nothing   *nothing would happen   they had done nothing they did nothing like so many others*   locked in the picture as the long arcs fell

 They were in Kew Gardens   in each other's arms skies flashed white and the day cracked open   stories smashed as all became one   through the glass flaming for a split-glass second all was transparent, the last light shone   glass became tears as the picture was taken

(George in Germany died a little earlier, by some irony thinking of Guy; still half believing goodness would win ... half believing, then not believing ... STARGATE   IMMORTALS
MORTALS, MORTALS   ALPHA   *I didn't*
TO OMEGA BASE   ... Angela and John in the same white second, half a mile apart, in the middle of a tiff ... Rose red and bare as in Frank's worst nightmare, drinking and weeping in her cooling bath ... Prunella bad-tempered on a bus to see her mother, *it's freezing, honestly, what was the point* ... Ray and his son in the shop with the corpses ... Joanna wheeled out in the garden of the Home, paralysed, staring at the dim lost sunlight .... Mr Briggs driving to the nearby churchyard with florist's roses as he did every week and his wife would not know he would never reach her, dry flowers powdered as the gravestone cracked ... Maisie killing turkeys for the Christmas season, worrying whether it would ever come ... Guy and his family rather later in Brisbane, scorched quite slowly, deprived of ozone ... Dr Akizuki giving blood to a patient, *the error shall not be made again* ... Frank in bliss on the side of the mountain, the word for miracle melting to nothing ...)

Some died instantly, some took time. Bags of skinned organs, spilling, crawling. A thing called *lethality*, a thing called time. Time was a measure of terror and pain   *no   I can't bear it please stop time*

The last light shone with no one to see it. The final photograph made its print. Everything was on it, nothing escaped. The pattern had an unearthly clarity. Melted eyeballs, shattering bone. Miracles of form became crackling bacon, miracles of feeling flashed to hot fat. Bleeding and terrified things pushed blindly against the pain which put out the light. *Some died instantly, most took time.* Nothing was too little for poison to reach it. Mice and sparrows found nowhere to hide. Black burst crusts which were rainbow fishes. Balls of burnt feathers on the burnt black ground. Flakes of ash were once soft moths quivering. Books in their charred skins feel less pain. ...

All was as if it had never   *tell me*
why is it dark already   what happened
why did we let our house burn down?

All was as if it had never been.

Blackening paper, the last leaves burning.

This poem was an entry in a poetry competition on the theme of nuclear weapons:

AUGUST 6, 1945

In the Enola Gay
five minutes before impact
he whistles a dry tune
Later he will say
that the whole blooming sky
went up like an apricot ice
Later he will laugh and tremble
at such a surrender,
for the eye of his belly
saw Marilyn's skirts
fly over her head forever

On the river bank
bees drizzle over
white hot rhododendrons
Later she will walk
the dust, a scarlet girl
with her whole stripped skin
at her heel, stuck like an old
shoe sole or mermaid's tail

Later she will lie down
in the flecked black ash
where the people are become
as lizards or salamanders
and, blinded, she will complain:
Mother you are late, so late

Later in dreams he will look
down shrieking and see
ladybirds
ladybirds

Alison Fell

- *Discuss your reactions to all you have read and looked at.*
- *An event like Hiroshima poses the problem for writers of expressing the almost unsayable; conventional ways of saying things are perhaps inadequate. Look closely at each extract and discuss what methods have been used to communicate in full the horror and significance of the Hiroshima blast.*
- *What are the strengths and limitations of the different media represented here?*
- *What differing political and cultural attitudes do you detect in these extracts?*

We are exposed to shocking images every day, and we know that they have a considerable effect on their audience. One of the factors which led to the end of the United States' involvement in Vietnam was the horrified reaction of viewers who saw the details of battle on their television screens each night. But there is a negative side to such exposure: years of begging-bowl images of starving children has perhaps desensitised us to their plight. We have seen it all before. Furthermore, we tend to see the starving as helpless victims, individual tragedies rather than the products of political and economic systems. We cannot tell from simply looking at a picture what has not been said, what was ignored, rejected or edited out. When the media presents a picture of the starving as passive pathetic victims, it can be difficult for the audience to reject its view. There are no windows on the world; we only get views of it from the media. All these comments apply equally to the written media. There is no truth independent of the way we interpret it. And we all interpret the world differently.

Reading List

Keywords by Raymond Williams (Flamingo, 1983) is an unusual dictionary of certain key words in our culture and explanations of how they have developed in meaning over the years.
Ways of Seeing by John Berger (BBC/Penguin, 1972) and *Another Way of Telling* by John Berger and Jean Mohr (Writers and Readers Publishing Cooperative, 1982) provide essential and stimulating reading about the relationship between medium, perception and culture with emphasis on the visual arts.
Language Change: Progress or Decay? by Jean Aitchison (Fontana Press, 1986) is full of fascinating examples of the changing, living language.

About Hiroshima
The Burning Book by Maggie Gee (Faber and Faber, 1985) is a novel which invites the reader to face the incalculable human loss of the next holocaust, interwoven with echoes of Hiroshima.
Hiroshima by John Hersey (Penguin, 1946) gives a Western view of Hiroshima.

THE VOICE OF REASON

THE ART OF REASON

Making sense is an art. To recruit the sympathy and support of the reader, a writer will make language work strongly in his or her favour. Readers should be alert to this persuasive aspect of language. Close study of language can reveal the way opinions and ideas are conveyed without declaring themselves.

On the surface the following extracts may seem to be fair comments, yet on reflection we may not share their logic. Here, for example, is a description of sisters from Jane Austen's novel *Persuasion*:

> A few years before, Anne Elliot had been a very pretty girl, but her bloom had vanished early; and as even in its height, her father had found little to admire in her, (so totally different were her delicate features and mild dark eyes from his own); there could be nothing in them now that she was faded and thin, to excite his esteem. He had never indulged much hope, he had now none, of ever reading her name in any other page of his favourite work. All equality of alliance must rest with Elizabeth; for Mary had merely connected herself with an old country family of respectability and large fortune, and had therefore *given* all the honour, and received none: Elizabeth would, one day or other, marry suitably.
>
> It sometimes happens, that a woman is handsomer at twenty-nine than she was ten years before; and, generally speaking, if there has been neither ill health nor anxiety, it is a time of life at which scarcely any charm is lost. It was so with Elizabeth; still the same handsome Miss Elliot that she had begun to be thirteen years ago; and Sir Walter might be excused, therefore, in forgetting her age, or, at least, be deemed only half a fool, for thinking himself and Elizabeth as blooming as ever, amidst the wreck of the good looks of every body else; for he could plainly see how old all the rest of his family and acquaintance were growing. Anne haggard, Mary coarse, every

face in the neighbourhood worsting; and the rapid increase of the crow's foot about Lady Russell's temples had long been a distress to him.

- *The description of the sisters is filtered to the reader through the eyes of their vain and critical father. Isolate which aspects of the language signal this filtering to the reader.*

Here is part of a poem by Alexander Pope called *Essay on Criticism*:

> Whoever thinks a faultless piece to see,
> Thinks what ne'er was, nor is, nor e'er shall be.
> In every work regard the writer's end,
> Since none can compass more than they intend;
> And if the means be just, the conduct true,
> Applause, in spite of trivial faults, is due.
> As men of breeding, sometimes men of wit,
> To avoid great errors, must the less commit,
> Neglect the rules each verbal critic lays,
> For not to know some trifles, is a praise.
> Most critics, fond of some subservient art,
> Still make the whole depend upon a part,
> They talk of principles, but notions prize,
> And all to one loved folly sacrifice.
>   Once on a time, la Mancha's knight, they say,
> A certain bard encountering on the way,
> Discoursed in terms as just, with looks as sage,
> As e'er could Dennis of the Grecian stage;
> Concluding all were desperate sots and fools,
> Who durst depart from Aristotle's rules.
> Our author, happy in a judge so nice,
> Produced his play, and begged the knight's advice,
> Made him observe the subject and the plot,
> The manners, passions, unities, what not?
> All which, exact to rule, were brought about,
> Were but a combat in the lists left out.
> 'What! leave the Combat out?' exclaims the knight;
> Yes, or we must renounce the Stagirite.
> 'Not so by Heaven' (he answers in a rage)
> 'Knights, squires, and steeds, must enter on the stage.'
> So vast a throng the stage can ne'er contain.
> 'Then build a new, or act it in a plain.'
>   Thus critics, of less judgment than caprice,
> Curious, not knowing, not exact, but nice,
> Form short ideas; and offend in arts
> (As most in manners) by a love to parts.

- *State the arguments put forward here in your own words, then provide a counter-argument to each one. Are Pope's arguments sound? Where do their weaknesses and their strengths lie?*

This article appeared in The Guardian on 7th April 1988:

The problem posed by viruses is growing, writes Rupert Goodwins

The power of infection

IT'S three in the morning. You've just finished 18 hours of programming, or maybe the last chapter of the book that will out-Archer Archer. Suddenly the computer screen clears and a message appears telling you to phone your bank and make a certain transaction. Fail to do so, the message continues, and your data files will be erased. And by the way, they've been scrambled already so don't try pulling the plug.

Your files are being held to ransom by a computer "virus". It's a nightmare, but it could happen. Worse, there may be no easy way of stopping it.

Consider: your masterwork is entrusted to hardware and software with a history so complex even the people who built them can't trace their genealogies more than two generations. The programmers who wrote your word processor used a language which had been written by programmers from another company. They, in turn, would have used another language, probably composed in yet a third. Assembler begets C begets application, each generation inheriting parts of its ancestor.

Yet other companies will have been involved in translating, duplicating and distributing all of this software — and anyone from any of them could have introduced a virus for their own eventual profit.

Although not a new idea, recent revelations about mischievous virus programs designed to hide for indefinite lengths of time, emerging only to damage data, have received wide publicity. Infected Commodore Amigas were the first machines to make the national newspapers (Computer Guardian, November 19) with Apple Macintosh and IBM PC viruses appearing more recently.

Today's strain of computer virus is liable to be a simple thing. A few hundred instructions, slipped into the tens of thousands that comprise a microcomputer's operating system, disrupt the normal run of events long enough to display a message and (just possibly) mangle a few files. An Amiga user might lose a game "borrowed" from a friend, or at worst a couple of hours of programming. In fact, a growing number are prepared to suffer the virus rather than a "cure" which excises a lot of harmless data along with the virus. So the rogue program is free to propagate, and nobody can be sure where it will end up.

But each development in the virus saga is merely a skirmish in an interminable war. On one side stand the forces of law, order and commercial interest. They want to protect their product, be that data, hardware or programs. On the other side are the hackers and crackers — individuals with an intimate understanding of the machinery and a supply of time and twisted ingenuity.

Once a new program appears, it's only a matter of time before the anti-copying schemes in it are "broken", and versions of the software start to change hands in the great grey barter market. As with illegal drugs, there are no guarantees sought or given. If a product fails to perform it is quietly forgotten, but a "useful" program can find its way onto thousands of discs in a very short time.

As cures for viruses are found, new and more virulent strains will be evolved. The possibilities are endless, and more than a little frightening given the availablity of the tools. It's as if a genetic engineering laboratory could be bought for a few hundred pounds at your local hi-fi shop.

It takes about ten minutes to sketch out the design for a virus program which lies dormant until it spots a certain set of conditions. It could be triggered by the presence on disc of a large data file updated daily, or of a set of text files which have grown steadily for the past two months. When the user next saves something to disc, the virus program takes control and encodes its target file.

And it's a simple step to take such an idea and hide it in a programming language which is passed on to friends and posted on bulletin boards. Once that's on a hard disc or network, all software becomes vulnerable.

The fact that Aldus shipped some US copies of its new Freehand program with a Macintosh virus shows that even the most famous names in the business could become unwitting carriers of some nasty surprise. And when a problem comes to light, the perpetrator may be impossible to trace. Dozens of people work on some programs, and changing jobs every year or so is not unusual in computing circles.

Worse, given that all untested program routines contain bugs, there's a good chance that when the virus finally appears it will behave in an unpredictable manner and nobody — not even the inventor — will be able to stop it.

A forgotten joke could reappear years later, like a recessive gene. The Bible has something to say about the sins of the fathers being vi-sited upon the sons, even unto the fourth generation. That's how it is with software.

Most of the above has already happened. A debugging program from a large American software company was partially written by a student on summer vacation work. As an afterthought he threw in a little routine to see if an illegal copy had been made. If it had, the computer displayed the message "The tree of evil bears bitter fruit. Now trashing hard disc". But there was a bug, and some time later a perfectly innocent user was accused, sentenced and punished.

What redress in law does the victim have? Given the international nature of software, tracing the original perpetrator, then proving guilt and intent will be difficult at best. There'll certainly be lucrative employment for the detectives of the data age, even if all they can do is find and erase the unwelcome fragments of code.

Doubtless at some point computerised analysis will be brought into play in an effort to establish purity. But somebody will have to write, duplicate and distribute the analysis programs . . .

- *Consider the aptness of the word 'virus' and study the way the analogy is developed. Pick out and comment upon the logic of this and other metaphors used in the article.*

We all listen critically to language when we think it will be biased, for example when we listen to advertisements or to politicians, but *all* words make subtle assumptions which we unwittingly accept as part of the language 'package'. For this reason it is important to attend closely to all kinds of language if we are to control our own opinions.

POLITICAL RHETORIC

I came, I saw, I conquered.

You turn if you want to; the lady's not for turning.

Government of the people, by the people, for the people.

Never in the field of human conflict has so much been owed to so many by so few.

- *Try paraphrasing these well quoted political lines to see where the impact of the original lies.*
- *What do you notice about the construction of these phrases?*
- *What other forms of writing do they have anything in common with: for example, adverts, slogans, catchphrases, proverbs, biblical sayings, jokes?*

Until the advent of television politics, the rhetoric of politicians was intended for oral delivery to large assemblies of people, such as mass meetings or Parliamentary debate. The oratorical tradition runs very deep in British politics, though many leaders now tailor their speeches to provide neat punchlines for the next news bulletin. Increasingly, however, politicians have to have 'media appeal' which means playing to the intimacy of the small screen and facial close-ups.

The following are examples of political rhetoric delivered in different contexts. Pay particular attention to the ways in which the language makes its impact.

This is the famous opening from Marx and Engels' *Communist Manifesto* of 1848:

> The history of all hitherto existing society is the history of class struggles.
>
> Freeman and slave, patrician and plebeian, lord and serf, guildmaster and journeyman, in a word, oppressor and oppressed, stood in constant opposition to one another, carried on an uninterrupted, now hidden, now open fight, a fight that each time ended, either in a revolutionary reconstitution of society at large, or in the common ruin of the contending classes.
>
> The modern bourgeois society that has sprouted from the ruins of feudal society has not done away with class antagonisms. It has but established new classes, new constitutions of oppression, new forms of struggle in place of old ones.
>
> Let the ruling classes tremble at a Communistic revolution. The proletarians have nothing to lose but their chains. They have a world to win.
>
> Working Men of All Countries, unite!

- *How has language been used here to rouse the reader and how do its features compare with the political slogans earlier?*

The following speech was delivered by the Prime Minister, Margaret Thatcher, to the House of Commons on the day after the Argentinian invasion of the Falkland Islands in April 1982:

> I am sure that the whole House will join me in condemning totally this unprovoked aggression by the Government of Argentina against British territory. [HON. MEMBERS: 'Hear, hear'.] It has not a shred of justification and not a scrap of legality.
>
> It was not until 8.30 this morning, our time, when I was able to speak to the governor, who had arrived in Uruguay, that I learnt precisely what had happened. He told me that the Argentines had landed at approximately 6 am Falkland's time, 10 am our time. One party attacked the capital from the landward side and another from the seaward side. The governor then sent a signal to us which we did not receive.
>
> Communications had ceased at 8.45 am our time. It is common for atmospheric conditions to make communications with Port Stanley difficult. Indeed, we had been out of contact for a period the previous night.
>
> The governor reported that the Marines, in the defence of Government House, were superb. He said that they acted in the best traditions of the

Royal Marines. They inflicted casualties, but those defending Government House suffered none. He had kept the local people informed of what was happening through a small local transmitter which he had in Government House. He is relieved that the islanders heeded his advice to stay indoors. Fortunately, as far as he is aware, there were no civilian casualties. When he left the Falklands, he said that the people were in tears. They do not want to be Argentine. He said that the islanders are still tremendously loyal. I must say that I have every confidence in the governor and the action that he took.

I must tell the House that the Falkland Islands and their dependencies remain British territory. No aggression and no invasion can alter that simple fact. It is the Government's objective to see that the islands are freed from occupation and are returned to British administration at the earliest possible moment.

Argentina has, of course, long disputed British sovereignty over the islands. We have absolutely no doubt about our sovereignty, which has been continuous since 1833. Nor have we any doubt about the unequivocal wishes of the Falkland Islanders, who are British in stock and tradition, and they wish to remain British in allegiance. We cannot allow the democratic rights of the islanders to be denied by the territorial ambitions of Argentina.

- *What view of the Argentinian invasion is presented here?*
- *How does the speech seek to persuade its audience to share the attitudes of its speaker?*
- *How does the style of the speech convey the authority of the speaker?*

The strike by the miners in 1984 saw unprecedented organisation by women in the mining communities in support of the action of their husbands. This speech was delivered at a Women's Rally in Barnsley in May of that year:

We cannot allow this Government to decimate our industry and our communities. Is this what we want for our kids?

In this country we aren't just separated as a class. We are separated as men and women. We, as women, have not often been encouraged to be involved actively in trade unions and organising. Organisation has always been seen as an area belonging to men. We are seen to be the domesticated element of a family. This for too many years has been the role expected of us. I have seen change coming for years and the last few weeks has seen it at its best. If this Government thinks its fight is only with the miners they are sadly mistaken. They are now fighting men, women and families.

I call today for solidarity from us all. We must stand firm and retain our self respect as a movement. I have only one message now and that is for Mrs Thatcher and her Government. Men, women and families are together now, and you've got a bloody fight on your hands. We are united and we will not be defeated. Not now. Not ever again.

- *What are the features of this speech which are designed to rouse support from its audience?*
- *How does the style compare with that of the speech by Mrs Thatcher?*
- *Compare the attitude of all three speeches towards their audiences.*

- *How far does the context of delivery determine style?*
- *What factors do you think are important in delivering an effective political speech? (Don't just think about the words used; think about the presentation, the body language etc.)*

ORATORY

It is often the delivery rather than the thought that makes one speaker more impressive than another. We tend to see people who are good speakers as either good thinkers or charismatic personalities – and charisma is something we are reluctant to define. All powerful and charismatic leaders have been aware of the importance of presentation techniques, from the Greek schools of oratory to Hitler's manipulation of applause or Ronald Reagan's use of the 'sincerity machine' – hidden screens which enable scripted speeches to be delivered more 'spontaneously' to an audience rather than read from a lectern. Political rhetoric is produced not only by the language of the speech but by the response of the audience: this is particularly true in an era when most people receive politics through television. The meaning that we take from a speech depends on the way it is reported to us.

The following analysis uses a passage from the last speech by the black civil rights leader, Martin Luther King, delivered the day before he was assassinated. King's audience were steeped in the style of the black churches of southern America.

- *First read this simple transcript:*

    And he's allowed me to go up to the mountain and I've looked over and I've seen the promised land. I may not get there with you but I want you to know tonight that we as a people will get to the promised land. So I'm happy tonight, I'm not worried, I'm not fearing any man – mine eyes have seen the glory of the coming of the lord.

- *Read this speech out loud and imagine where you would pause or emphasise and how the audience might be expected to respond.*
- *Now examine the analysis of the speech. You will need to refer to the explanation of the symbols.*

Example	Explanation
AUDIENCE: XXXXXXXXX	Loud applause
AUDIENCE: xxxxxxxxx	Quiet applause
(0.5) (.)	Numbers indicate pause lengths to nearest tenth of a second. Dot indicates micropause (less than 0.2 seconds)
hhh	In-breath or out-breath – the more h's the longer the duration
I <u>say</u> to y ↑ <u>OU</u>	Capital letters indicate more loudly spoken particles. Underlining indicates extra emphasis

KING:	... AND HE'S ALLOWED ME TO GO UP TO THE MOUNTAIN (0.5)
AUDIENCE:	Go ahea ⌐ d
KING:	└ AND I'VE LOOKED OVER
AUDIENCE:	Yeah
KING:	AND I'VE SEEN (0.4) THE PROMISED LA ⌐ ND
AUDIENCE:	└ Holy ⌐ Holy Holy Holy
AUDIENCE:	└ Ame ⌐ n
KING:	└ I MAY NOT GET THERE WITH YOU
AUDIENCE:	Yah-ha ⌐ hah
AUDIENCE:	└ Hol ⌐ y
KING:	└ BUT I WANT YOU TO KNOW TONIGHT
AUDIENCE:	Yeahh ⌐ hhh
KING:	└ THAT WE AS A ⌐ PEOPLE
AUDIENCE:	└ Yeahhhhhhh
KING:	WILL GET TO THE PROMISED LAN ⌐ D
AUDIENCE:	└ Yeah ⌐ hh (6.0)
AUDIENCE:	└ xxXXXXX ⌐ XXXxxxxx-xxxxxx-x ⌐
KING:	└ SO I'M HAPPY ┘ TONIGHT

I'M NOT <u>WORRIED</u>
I'M NOT FEARING <u>ANY</u> MAN –
<u>MINE EYES</u> HAVE SEEN THE
GLOR ⌐ Y (.) OF THE <u>COMING</u> OF THE
<u>LORD</u> └

AUDIENCE:	└ Yea ⌐ hhhhhhhhhhhhhhhhhhhhhh ....
AUDIENCE:	└ xxxXXXXXXXXXXXXXXX ....

(from *Our Master's Voices* by Max Atkinson)

- *What insights does this offer on the delivery and reception of King's words? Has your understanding of their meaning changed between the two readings?*

THE VOICE OF COMMON SENSE

In the extract below the eighteenth century writer, Jonathan Swift is offering what he describes as 'A Modest Proposal' to deal with the problem of child poverty in Ireland. As you read it, note how you respond to the language of the argument:

A MODEST PROPOSAL

for preventing the Children of Poor People from being a Burthen to their Parents, or the Country, and for making them Beneficial to the Publick.

It is a melancholly Object to those, who walk through this great Town, or travel in the Country, when they see the *Streets*, the *Roads*, and *Cabbin-Doors*, crowded with *Beggars* of the female Sex, followed by three, four, or six Children, *all in Rags*, and importuning every Passenger for an Alms. These *Mothers* instead of being able to work for their modest livelyhood, are forced to employ all their time in Stroling, to beg Sustenance for their *helpless Infants*, who, as they grow up, either turn *Thieves* for want of work, or leave their *dear native Country to fight for the Pretender in Spain*, or sell themselves to the *Barbadoes*.

I think it is agreed by all Parties, that this prodigious number of Children, in the Arms, or on the Backs, or at the *heels* of their *Mothers*, and frequently of their *Fathers*, is *in the present deplorable state of the Kingdom*, a very great additional grievance; and therefore whoever could find out a fair, cheap and easy method of making these Children sound and useful Members of the commonwealth would deserve so well of the publick, as to have his Statue set up for a preserver of the Nation.

But my Intention is very far from being confined to provide only for the Children of *professed Beggars*: It is of a much greater extent, and shall take in the whole number of Infants at a certain Age, who are born of Parents in effect as little able to support them, as those who demand our Charity in the Streets.

As to my own part, having turned my thoughts, for many Years, upon this important Subject, and maturely weighed the several *Schemes of other Projectors*, I have always found them grossly mistaken in their computation. It is true a Child, *just dropt from it's Dam*, may be supported by her Milk, for a Solar year with little other Nourishment, at most not above the Value of two Shillings, which the Mother may certainly get, or the Value in *Scraps*, by her lawful Occupation of begging, and it is exactly at one year Old that I propose to provide for them, in such a manner, as, instead of being a Charge upon their *Parents*, or the *Parish*, or *wanting Food and Raiment* for the rest of their Lives, they shall, on the Contrary, contribute to the Feeding and partly to the Cloathing of many Thousands.

There is likewise another great Advantage in my Scheme, that it will prevent those *voluntary Abortions*, and that horrid practice of *Women murdering their Bastard Children*, alas! too frequent among us, Sacrificing the *poor innocent Babes*, I doubt, more to avoid the Expence, than the Shame, which would move Tears and Pity in the most Savage and inhuman breast.

The number of Souls in this Kingdom being usually reckoned one Million and a half, Of these I calculate there may be about two hundred thousand Couple whose Wives are Breeders, from which number I Substract thirty Thousand Couples, who are able to maintain their own Children, although I apprehend there cannot be so many under *the present distresses of the Kingdom*, but this being granted, there will remain an hundred and seventy thousand Breeders. I again Substract fifty Thousand for those Women who miscarry, or whose Children dye by accident, or disease within the Year. There only remain an hundred and twenty thousand Children of poor Parents annually born: The question therefore is, how this number shall be reared, and provided for, which, as I have already said, under the present Situation of Affairs, is utterly impossible by all the methods hitherto proposed, for we can *neither employ them in Handicraft*, or *Agriculture*; we neither build Houses, (I mean in the Country) nor cultivate Land: They can very seldom pick up a Livelihood *by Stealing* till they arrive at six years Old, except where they are of towardly parts, although, I confess they learn the Rudiments much earlier, during which time, they can however be properly looked upon only as *Probationers*, as I have been informed by a principal Gentleman in the County of *Cavan*, who protested to me, that he never knew above one or two Instances under the Age of six, even in a part of the Kingdom *so renowned for the quickest proficiency in that Art.*

I am assured by our Merchants, that a Boy or Girl, before twelve years Old, is no saleable Commodity, and even when they come to this Age, they will not yield above three Pounds, or three Pounds and half a Crown at most on the Exchange, which cannot turn to Account either to the Parents or the Kingdom, the Charge of Nutriment and Rags having been at least four times that Value.

I shall now therefore humbly propose my own thoughts, which I hope will not be lyable to the least Objection.

I have been assured by a very knowing *American* of my acquaintance in *London*, that a young healthy Child well Nursed is at a year Old a most delicious, nourishing, and wholesome Food, whether *Stewed, Roasted, Baked,* or *Boyled*, and I make no doubt that it will equally serve in a *Fricasie*, or a *Ragoust.*

I do therefore humbly offer it to *publick consideration*, that of the hundred and twenty thousand Children, already computed, twenty thousand may be reserved for Breed, whereof only one fourth part to be Males, which is more than we allow to *Sheep, black Cattle,* or *Swine*, and my reason is that these Children are seldom the Fruits of Marriage, *a Circumstance not much regarded by our Savages*, therefore *one Male* will be sufficient to serve *four Females*. That the remaining hundred thousand may at a year Old be offered in Sale to the *persons of Quality*, and *Fortune*, through the Kingdom, always advising the Mother to let them Suck plentifully in the last Month, so as to render them Plump, and Fat for a good Table. A Child will make two Dishes at an Entertainment for Friends, and when the Family dines alone, the fore or hind Quarter will make a reasonable Dish, and seasoned with a little Pepper or Salt will be very good Boiled on the fourth Day, especially in Winter.

- *How 'modest' is this proposal?*
- *What do you think are the writer's views of the situation in Ireland, and at what point in your reading did you feel you had established them?*
- *What do you notice about the way the argument is constructed and how it positions the reader?*
- *Swift's piece is a famous example of an outrageous idea being presented in the language of reasonable common sense. But what do we understand by 'common sense'?*
- *In what circumstances do people appeal to or buy claim to 'common sense'?*

Common sense is a popular notion based on the democratic ideal – a natural quality shared by sensible citizens to be set against the 'theories' of the intellectual or radical. It is apparently uncontroversial and apolitical, but nonetheless it is appropriated by all political viewpoints. A lot of important decisions are finally referred to common sense – as voters or members of a jury making crucial judgements we are urged to use it – so it is important to recognise the possibility that we can construct common sense just as we can construct any other viewpoint. Some might argue, for example, that it is common sense that a mother wants to stay with her child, while others might see this as social conditioning rather than a 'natural' response. Skilful use of language can persuade us that an attitude is so straightforward that it is unquestionable.

The following extract is from a speech by Margaret Thatcher, made in 1980. The 'winter of discontent' was a popular media term for the industrial unrest of 1979 which led to the Conservative defeat of the Labour government. Consider the meaning of 'common sense' in this passage and how the speaker suggests it is achieved:

> If our people feel they are part of a great nation and are prepared to will the means to keep it great, then a great nation we shall be and shall remain.
>
> So what could stop us achieving that? What then stands in our way? The prospects of another winter of discontent? I suppose it might, but I prefer to believe that certain lessons have been learnt from experience, that we are coming slowly, painfully to an autumn of understanding. I hope it will be followed by a winter of common sense.
>
> If it is not, we shall not be diverted from our course. To those waiting with baited breath for that favourite media catch-phrase, the U-turn, I have only one thing to say: You turn if you want; the lady's not for turning.

While we often recognise the techniques of the professional persuaders such as politicians and advertisers, we tend not to view ordinary social interaction in the same way. Yet 'common sense' is a social phenomenon, a way of viewing our world that the vast majority are expected to share.

This homely advice is taken from a popular magazine. Consider how useful it is, and what purpose it serves:

> Growing up is never easy, and both parents must learn when not to intrude. They should let their children know that they are always there to listen and help, but not ask too many questions, as this is likely to send a child back into his or her shell. It's better if they wait until the child is ready to confide the growing up pains – whether it be a son's worries about an exam or interview, or a daughter's first love. The old clichés like, 'It's not the end of the world' or 'You'll get over it' or 'There's plenty more fish in the sea' are true enough, but not necessarily what a worried or heartbroken teenager wants to hear. A good heart-to-heart with a loving parent who really understands and listens is the balm they really need.
>
> Needless to say, there has to be a happy medium between pouring out your sorrows to everyone you meet and being 'boxed in', unable or unwilling to confide. But finding that medium is particularly hard for a child brought up in one of those homes where things which really matter to them are never brought out into the open. They are being denied the special good fortune which any family has within its power to bestow – to be part of a united, loving and supportive band of friends.

- *What assumptions does the writer make about human nature and behaviour (such as relationships between the sexes or within the family)?*
- *For both these examples of 'common sense', examine the ways in which the language assumes agreement in the reader or listener.*

Reading List

Political Rhetoric
Political rhetoric is usually best savoured in the form of live speeches. Elections bring out the best one-liners but party conferences are the place to find the old traditions of oratorical performance. If it is not conference season, try:
Writings on the Wall by Tony Benn (Faber and Faber, 1984) – an anthology of radical speeches and statements: rousing stuff.
Hansard – the transcript of parliamentary debates, usually kept for inspection at big libraries, and more entertaining than you expect.
Our Master's Voice by Max Atkinson (Routledge, 1989) which analyses political speeches.

Feminist Criticism
Feminist Literary Theory (ed.) Mary Eagleton (Basil Blackwell, 1986) contains some accessible extracts covering a wide range of issues.
On Gender and Writing (ed.) M. Wandor (Pandora Press, 1983).

A QUESTION OF TASTE

SOCIAL VALUES

- *Read through the following extracts, considering whether, and for what reasons, a reader might find them offensive:*

I MACDUFF: What three things does drink especially provoke?

PORTER: Marry, sir, nose-painting, sleep and urine. Lechery, sir, it provokes and unprovokes; it provokes the desire, but it takes away the performance: therefore much drink may be said to be an equivocator with lechery: it makes him and it mars him; it sets him on and it takes him off; it persuades him and it disheartens him; makes him stand to and not stand to; in conclusion, equivocates him in a sleep, and giving him the lie, leaves him.

(from Shakespeare's *Macbeth*)

2 That night I lay with Jesus, held in his arms, in a grain store belonging to a kindly farmer whose property lay along our route. Separated from the others by only the wall of the cloak he cast about us, we touched each other in the darkness. As we drew closer and closer towards each other we entered a new place, a country of heat and sweetness and light different to the ground we had explored together before. I felt us taken upwards and transformed: I no longer knew what was inside and what was outside, where he ended and I began, only that our bones and flesh and souls were suddenly woven up together in a great melting and pouring. I was six years old again, lying on the roof looking up at the stars, at the rents in the dark fabric of the sky and the light shining through it. Only this time I rose, I pierced through the barrier of shadow, and was no longer an I, but part of a great whirl of light that throbbed and rang with music – for a moment, till I was pulled back by the sound of my own voice whispering words I did not understand: this is the resurrection, and the life.

(from *The Wild Girl* by Michele Roberts)

3 Noddy had five dear little passengers one afternoon. They were all small
pink rabbits with ribbons round their necks.

They were going to have a picnic on Bluebell Hill, and they had a basket
of food with them. What fun they were going to have!

Noddy set them down on the hill. 'I'll come and fetch you at half-past
five,' he said. 'Have a nice time!'

At a quarter past five he set off in his car to fetch them. On his way he
passed a small black golliwog, sitting at the side of the road, with a basket
beside him. He was just stuffing a big bun into his mouth when Noddy
passed.

'Somebody else having a picnic,' thought Noddy. 'I'll ask Big-Ears if he'll
have one with me tomorrow.'

Now, before he reached Bluebell Hill what did he see but all the five pink
rabbits hiding under a hedge, looking as scared as could be. He stopped his
car at once, and they came running over to him.

'Oh, Noddy, Noddy! We're so glad you've come! Have you seen the fox?'

'What fox? No, of course not,' said Noddy. 'Why? What's happened?'

'Oh dear! We were just going up to begin our picnic when a golliwog came
running up, calling out "Fox! Fox! He's looking for rabbits! Beware!" So we
had to leave our picnic and run away!'

'You poor little things,' said Noddy, very sorry for them. Then he
suddenly remembered the golliwog he had seen picnicking by the road. Oh,
the bad little thing! He must have called out 'Fox!' just to frighten the
rabbits, and then taken their picnic things!

Noddy looked very fierce. He would punish that mean golly. He packed
the little rabbits into his car and drove them home.

(from *The New Big Noddy Book* by Enid Blyton)

These examples have been the subject of censorship or controversy at
different times. Few people would now consider expurgating the works
of Shakespeare or Chaucer to render them suitable for schools, but the
'cleaning up' of the classics became quite an industry in the Victorian
era. We tend to see ourselves as much more liberal today: the trial in
1960 when the jury found *Lady Chatterley's Lover* by D. H. Lawrence
not guilty of obscenity is often seen as a turning point in the relationship
between literature and morality. Obviously society's view of what is
offensive is subject to change: what entertains one century might offend
the next. A Victorian might be revolted by the eighteenth century's
enjoyment of the subject of farting. A 1980s feminist might be offended
by the fiction of sexual liberation from the 1960s.

While the relationship between culture and morality is clearly
inextricable and ever-shifting, there is a demand for the institutions in
our society such as the law, government, education and media to define
boundaries of acceptability for public taste. One attempt to deal with
this problem is to distinguish between 'taste' and 'standards', as did this
BBC document:

That taste is ephemeral is demonstrated several times in the life of a generation which will see its clothes, its wallpaper, its ornaments, pass in and out of fashion and possibly return to favour within a few years. Taste may be defined as a matter of manners which reflects the prevailing sense of what is done and not done between individuals. Standards have a greater permanence, reflecting a continuing view that certain things are good, should be promoted and defended, because they conform to a particular view of the relationship between the individual and society, the aggregate of the individuals in it.

- *Bearing these definitions in mind, draw up a charter for a new television channel or publishing house to explain your company's policy on taste, covering such areas as language, race, religion, sexuality, violence and censorship.*
- *What difficulties did you encounter in devising the charter? What issues were most difficult to resolve and why?*
- *Do you agree with the distinction made in the BBC document between taste and standards?*
- *How necessary do you think such guidelines are? What advantages/ disadvantages do they offer? Is it possible for media such as television, film and literature to function without any concept of standards?*

MINDING LANGUAGE

- *Read carefully through this description of the slaughter of a cow:*

The son pushes a spring through the hole in the skull into the cow's brain. It goes in nearly twenty centimetres. He agitates it to be sure that all the animal's muscles will relax, and pulls it out. The mother holds the uppermost foreleg by the fetlock in her two hands. The son cuts by the throat and the blood floods out on to the floor. For a moment it takes the form of an enormous velvet skirt, whose tiny waist band is the lip of the wound. Then it flows on and resembles nothing.

Life is liquid. The Chinese were wrong to believe that the essential was breath. Perhaps the soul is breath. The cow's pink nostrils are still quivering. Her eye is staring unseeing, and her tongue is falling out of the side of her mouth.

When the tongue is cut out, it will be hung beside the head and the liver. All the heads, tongues and livers are hanging in a row together. The jaws gape open, tongueless, and each circular set of teeth is smeared with a little blood, as though the drama had begun with an animal, which was not carnivorous, eating flesh. Underneath the livers on the concrete floor are spots of bright vermilion blood, the colour of poppies when they first blossom, before they deepen and become crimson. [. . .]

The peasant to whom the cow belongs comes over to the pram to point out why she had to be slaughtered; two of her teats were decomposing and she was almost impossible to milk. He picks up a teat in his hand. It is as warm as in the stable when he milked her. The mother and son listen to him, nod, but do not reply and do not stop working.

The son severs and twists off the four hoofs and throws them into a wheelbarrow. The mother removes the udder. Then, through the cut hide, the son axes the breast bone. This is similar to the last axing of a tree before it falls, for from that moment onwards, the cow, no longer an animal, is transformed into meat, just as the tree is transformed into timber.

- *How did you react to the subject matter, language and narrative style of this piece?*

I come home after three fucking years in fucking Africa, and what do I fucking well find? – my wife in bed, engaging in illicit cohabitation with a male!

(quoted in Richard Hoggart's introduction to *Lady Chatterley's Lover*)

The words that shock so much at first don't shock at all after a while. Is this because the mind is depraved by habit? Not a bit. It is that the words merely shocked the eye, they never shocked the mind at all ... People with minds realise that they aren't shocked, and never really were: and they experience a sense of relief.

D. H. Lawrence

Can certain words be 'wrong' in themselves? Is it simply the social convention of the time, or the use to which they are put that renders them harmful? Words describing genitalia would be seen as appropriate in a medical text but what about a novel or TV drama that features a scene with a doctor? Words which we consider vulgar today, *arse* or *shit* for example, used to be perfectly acceptable English: words assume the respectable or offensive character society allots them.

- *In what situations do you exercise restraint in the language you speak or write?*
- *In what circumstances do you consider profane or obscene language to be appropriate or justified?*

The poet Tony Harrison made a television broadcast of his long poem 'V' in 1987. This caused considerable controversy in the press at the time, because of the language of the poem. The form of the poem recalls the famous eighteenth century elegy by Thomas Grey in which the poet figure in a churchyard contemplates death and an imaginary encounter with a simple rural 'swain'. Harrison's graveyard, where his parents are buried, is situated above an old pit and the poem takes place in 1984, the time of the miners' strike. Read this extract from the poem carefully, considering its use of language. You might do this by annotating the poem, marking different patterns or groups of words in different colours.

This graveyard stands above a worked-out pit,
Subsidence makes the obelisks all list.

One leaning left's marked FUCK, one right's marked SHIT
sprayed by some peeved supporter who was pissed.

Far-sighted for his family's future dead,
but for his wife, this banker's still alone
on his long obelisk, and doomed to head
a blackened dynasty of unclaimed stone,

now graffitied with a crude four-letter word.
His children and grandchildren went away
and never came back home to be interred,
so left a lot of space for skins to spray.

The language of this graveyard ranges from
a bit of Latin for a former Mayor
or those who laid their lives down at the Somme,
the hymnal fragments and the gilded prayer,

how people 'fell asleep in the Good Lord',
brief chisellable bits from the good book
and rhymes whatever length they could afford,
to CUNT, PISS, SHIT and (mostly) FUCK!

. . . .

But why inscribe these *graves* with CUNT and SHIT?
Why choose neglected tombstones to disfigure?
This pitman's of last century daubed PAKI GIT,
this grocer Broadbent's aerosolled with NIGGER?

They're there to shock the living, not arouse
the dead from their deep peace to lend support
for the causes skinhead spraycans could espouse.
The dead would want their desecrators caught!

Jobless though they are how can these kids,
even though their team's lost one more game,
believe that the 'Pakis', 'Niggers', even 'Yids'
sprayed on the tombstones here should bear the blame?

What is it that these crude words are revealing?
What is it that this aggro act implies?
Giving the dead their xenophobic feeling
or just a *cri-de-coeur* because man dies?

So what's a cri-de-coeur, *cunt? Can't you speak*
the language that yer mam spoke. Think of 'er!
Can yer only get yer tongue round fucking greek?
Go and fuck yourself with cri-de-coeur.

'She didn't talk like you do for a start!'
I shouted, turning where I thought the voice had been.
She didn't understand yer fucking 'art'!
She thought yer fucking poetry obscene!

I wish on this skin's word deep aspirations,
first the prayer for my parents I can't make,

then a call to Britain and to all nations
made in the name of love for peace's sake.

- *How do you react to this extract?*
- *What did you notice about the types of language in the poem?*
- *What does the poem seem to be saying about language and about poetry?*
- *How would you assess the appropriateness of this poem*
  a) *for broadcast on television?*
  b) *for use as an A level text?*

SEX

The representation of sex in literature is influenced by the changing attitudes of society. Sex was a taboo subject in nineteenth century literature compared to the more liberal or explicit treatments of much twentieth century writing. At the same time pornography and prostitution were widespread in the nineteenth century, and this fact is used to support the popularly held belief of contemporary society that repression has adverse consequences, and that we in the twentieth century have got the balance about right.

Many people believe (and indeed this is expressed in our laws) that there is a line to be drawn between the explicit and the obscene. Artistic merit is often used as a defence against the charge of obscenity. The problems here are that it is difficult to establish that a work has a corrupting influence and it is equally difficult to define the notion of artistic worth. The final appeal is often to 'common sense', which, as an earlier chapter (The Voice of Reason) has suggested, is itself both questionable and subject to change.

Just as some people see pornography as the result of widespread sexual repression, others equate it with sexual liberation and sexual explicitness. Feminists, however, have argued that there is nothing natural in the expression of pornography and that it cannot liberate the full extent of human sexual desires. Rather, it is seen as an expression of man's hatred and fear of the 'other', usually woman.

The following passages from novels deal with sexual encounters.

His hands and his mouth were slow and electric and his body in my arms was tenderly fierce.

Afterwards he told me that when the moment came I screamed. I didn't know I had. I only knew that a chasm of piercing sweetness suddenly opened and drowned me and that I dug my nails into his hips to make sure of taking him with me. Then he sleepily said some sweet things and kissed me once and his body slithered away and lay still and I stayed on my back and gazed up into the red darkness and listened to his breathing. [. . .]

I think I know why I gave myself so completely to this man, how I was capable of it with someone I had met only six hours before. Apart from the excitement of his looks, his authority, his maleness, he had come from nowhere, like the prince in the fairytales, and he had saved me from the dragon. But for him, I would now be dead, after suffering God knows what before. He could have changed the wheel on his car and gone off, or, when danger came, he could have saved his own skin. But he had fought for my life as if it had been his own. And then, when the dragon was dead, he had taken me as his reward. In a few hours, I knew, he would be gone – without protestations of love, without apologies or excuses. And that would be the end of that – gone, finished.

All women love semi-rape. They love to be taken. It was his sweet brutality against my bruised body that had made the act of love so piercingly wonderful. That and the coinciding of nerves completely relaxed after the removal of tension and danger, the warmth of gratitude, and a woman's natural feeling for her hero. I had no regrets and no shame. There might be many consequences for me – not the least that I might now be dissatisfied with other men. But whatever my troubles were, he would never hear of them. I would not pursue him and try to repeat what there had been between us. I would stay away from him and leave him to go his own road where there would be other women, countless other women, who would probably give him as much physical pleasure as he had with me. I wouldn't care, or at least I told myself that I wouldn't care, because none of them would ever own him – own any larger piece of him than I now did. And for all my life I would be grateful to him, for everything. And I would remember him for ever as my image of a man.

(from The Spy Who Loved Me by Ian Fleming)

This extract from a novel deals with the relationship of Helen and Robert:

This was being together, and it was also circling around each other before they engaged, their arms tying each other up like string around parcels that only their movements asleep will undo, their tongues licking at skin that does not dissolve like sugar, but remains instead endlessly renewed and enjoying. They feel a mixture of pleasure, being in the right place, which means together, and great nervousness. How different are they from one another? How much does it matter? The sex is to explore that.

Now Adam too, and not only Eve, is allowed to be curious, to want to find out, with no slapping-down or needing to blame afterwards. He can discover her, how her lips curl, just so, in a certain way, how her tissues inside are ribbed and soft, how her breasts rise and fall, how her nipples are brown and pink and sturdy like raspberries, how she rises, all of her, how her deep heart comes right out to meet him and take him in.

And now Eve can look at Adam with desire, she can describe him with words and summon up images, no longer silent. His skin, she tells him, is the colour of apricots, and breathes with the smells of spices and earth when her mouth moves across it. She praises his short black hair, which has silver threads in it, and smells of sweat and of sun, and his thumbnails, which are lined with sweet green dirt. She celebrates him, all his beauty, part by part, and the whole, she sings of him standing up to greet her and wave at her, and she holds him, and takes him in.

There are no words in the language to describe her embrace of him, and so they are forced to become poets, giggling, inventing new ones. This is what Helen's mother meant, then, when she used to say: it is very beautiful. When a man darts like a humming-bird and leaps like a salmon, and a woman flies up and out to meet him, and encloses him in mid-air, in the depths of streams. Only Helen, convinced she was a sinner, did not want to remember, did not want to know. But now there are words, and words, which flash across the darkness of her mind. Doors open, close, along the corridor. She is a violent, a blue flower, that beats its fleshy wings, that claps, she is a drum of blood, a shout, a city street. She presses down and down and down, as waves of blue sensation eddy up and up and up.

Robert is letting her move him down strange paths, to places where they have not been together before. He lets her guide him, he listens to what her body says, he follows her slow dance, learning new steps very different from his former ones, a gentler rhythm. They let the body take over. Their bodies decline for them the verb to be: I am, you are, he is, she is. We are. And Helen comes, comes in response to him who responds to her, and is no longer frightened of you, me, and can let her body say with his: we are.

(from *The Visitation* by Michele Roberts)

- *Examine the language used in connection with sex in these passages. What do you notice?*
- *What is suggested in these pieces about the sexuality of men and women, and how is it conveyed to the reader?*
- *Do you find either of these extracts offensive?*

FREE SPEECH

- *What does freedom of expression mean?*
- *Does every group or individual have equal access and equal right to free speech?*
- *Are there any areas where it is necessary to restrict freedom of speech? Why?*
- *Consider the following possibilities for publication and the issues raised by them to discuss society's capacity for free speech:*
  - *a) the autobiography of an ex-civil servant in which she reveals ways in which the government of the time concealed information about a national crisis from the public and House of Commons;*
  - *b) the circulation in schools and public libraries of a novel for children featuring a homosexual relationship between two teenagers;*
  - *c) a novel features passages which are considered profoundly offensive to a religious culture which threatens considerable political unrest if the novel is not banned.*

A people which is able to say everything becomes able to do everything.

Napoleon

> We need to understand the paradox that language is both potentially
> liberating and potentially enslaving.
>
> Harold Rosen

Freedom of speech is deeply embedded within our idea of liberty. It is held to be a fundamental human right to be cherished and upheld in a democratic society: it sets us apart from countries which exercise censorship and repress dissenting voices, such as the USSR or South Africa. A civilisation which burns books, like Hitler's Germany, must, so the argument goes, be profoundly corrupt, and the health of a society is indicated by its relationship with art.

The relationship between art and politics is complex. Like taste, which we suggested earlier was subject to the changing attitudes of society, what is considered dangerous or subversive will also vary and be closely tied in with social and political beliefs and controls. We tend to isolate art as an aesthetic matter, the privilege and indulgence of a free society. Politics is treated as a practical matter. The relationship between the two emerges when we consider the controls which exist to curb abuses of free speech. Legislation is based on the belief that we are deeply affected by the cultural artefacts we encounter. If art can enhance life and be morally uplifting, then it can also degrade and corrupt. But then, how can we explain the evidence pointed to by George Steiner, that Nazis who committed atrocities in the concentration camps went home in the evenings to enjoy Shakespeare and classical music?

We have to question our trust in the humanising effect of art, the belief that it is good for us, just as we need to question whether free speech is always liberating. What we can say and the ways we can say it are not a simple matter of how accurately our language can match our intended meaning; neither is our response to literature aroused in a vacuum – both trivial questions of taste and profound responses of outrage are aspects of the political as well as of the personal world.

Reading List

Controversial Works
There are many controversial writers, but the following examples were the subject of public debate which you can research:
D. H. Lawrence's *Lady Chatterley's Lover* (Penguin, 1969) – a trial in 1960 supported the publishers, Penguin, in their argument that it was not pornographic, but had artistic merit and should be published. There are interesting comments in Lawrence's essays (e.g. 'On Obscenity').
We have already mentioned Tony Harrison's poem '*V*' (Bloodaxe Books, 1985). The televised production in 1987 provoked many

protests. Ironically, language itself is the subject of the poem.

Son of Man, a television play by Dennis Potter, attempted to show the human side of Christ and was severely criticised. His other plays are equally provocative.

Howard Brenton's *Romans in Britain* (Methuen, 1982) was a play shown at the National Theatre. It was prosecuted because of a male rape scene, but the charge was dropped.

D. M. Thomas's *The White Hotel* (Penguin, 1988) is a controversial novel in many ways, for its sexuality, portrait of Freud and depiction of Nazi violence.

Critical Works

For considering the issue of pornography, Susan Griffin's book *Pornography and Silence* (The Woman's Press, 1981) is very interesting. Kate Millet's feminist look at male writers on sex, such as Henry Miller, in *Sexual Politics* (Virago, 1977) is a famous and provocative analysis. Few women venture into pornography. Try Kathy Acker, *Blood and Guts in High School* (Picador, 1984).